The History of
Buddhism in India

The History of Buddhism in India

by

KHENCHEN
THRANGU RINPOCHE

Oral Translation of Chapters 1 - 8
by Ken and Katia Holmes
and
Cornelia Weishaar-Günter

Translation of Chapters 9 - 12
by Jules Levinson

*Zhyisil Chokyi Ghatsal Charitable Trust
Publications*

Acknowledgment

We would like to thank the many persons who helped make this book possible.

First, we would like to express our sincere thanks and appreciation to Khabje Khenchen Thrangu Rinpoche for his great compassion and wisdom in bestowing these precious teachings. For chapters one to eight, we would like to thank Ken and Katia Holmes for translating this work, Margot Neuman for transcribing the tapes and Jean Johnson for editing the manuscript and Cornelia Weishaar-Gunter for going through this manuscript and the original Tibetan tapes and correcting them. For chapters nine to twelve, we wish to thank Jules Levinson for translating and Gaby Hollmann for editing them. For chapter thirteen, Kai Jensen for all his work in researching these sites and editing throughout the book.

Our thanks also go to Sangye for additional material, Laurie and Judy Renier and Dr. Heather Buttle for proofreading and Clark Johnson for his tireless ongoing efforts in making the publication of Thrangu Rinpoche's teachings possible.

May this supreme, peerless teaching,
The precious treasure of the Victorious Ones,
Spread and extend throughout the world
Like the sun shining in the sky.

Copyrighted © 2008
Namo Buddha Publications &
Zhyisil Chokyi Ghatsal Charitable Trust

This book is copyright. Apart from any fair dealing for the purpose of private study, research, criticism or review as permitted under the Copyright Act 1968, no part of this book may be stored or reproduced by any process without prior written permission. Enquiries should be made to the publisher.

Namo Buddha Publications Publications
1390 Kalmia Avenue, Boulder, CO 80304-1813
Clark@NamoBuddhaPublications.com / www.namobuddhapublications.com

&

Zhyisil Chokyi Ghatsal Charitable Trust Publications
PO Box 6259 Wellesley Street, Auckland, New Zealand
inquiries@greatliberation.org / www.greatliberation.org

National Library of New Zealand Cataloguing-in-Publication Data

Thrangu, Rinpoche, 1933-
The development of Buddhism in India / by Khabje Khenchen Thrangu Rinpoche; oral translation of chapters 1 - 8 by Ken and Katia Holmes; retranslated by Cornelia Weishaar-Günter; translation of chapters 9 -12 by Jules Levinson.
Includes index.
ISBN 978-1-877294-39-6
1. Buddhism—India. I. Holmes, Ken. II. Holmes, Katia.
III. Weishaar-Günter, Cornelia. IV. Levinson, Jules B.
V. Title.
294.30954—dc 22

Cover photo: Ashoka pillar in bodhi leaf
Note: Tibetan words are given as they are pronounced, not spelled in Tibetan. Their actual spelling can be found in the Glossary of Tibetan words.

Table of Contents

Foreword by Venerable Choje Lama Shedrup   11

Chapter 1
THE LIFE OF THE BUDDHA   13

Chapter 2
THE THREE WHEELS OF DHARMA   21

Chapter 3
THE SECOND AND THIRD DHARMA COUNCILS   31

Chapter 4
THE MAHAYANA AND THE VAJRAYANA COUNCILS   37

Chapter 5
THE FOUNDATION VEHICLE PATH   43

Chapter 6
THE MAHAYANA PATH   51

Chapter 7
THE SPREAD OF THE VAJRAYANA TEACHINGS   65

Chapter 8
THE TEN BUDDHIST SCIENCES — 73

Chapter 9
BODHGAYA AND THE BUDDHA ESSENCE — 83

Chapter 10
SARNATH AND THE FOUR NOBLE TRUTHS — 95

Chapter 11
KUSHINAGAR AND IMPERMANENCE — 123

Chapter 12
LUMBINI AND THE EXCELLENT DHARMA — 135

Chapter 13
BUDDHIST PILGRIMAGE SITES — 153
by Kai Jensen

Introduction — 153
Eight Major Sites — 157
  Lumbini — 158
  Bodhgaya — 161
  Sarnath — 163
  Rajgir — 165
  Shravasti — 169
  Sankashya — 173
  Nalanda — 174
  Kushinagar — 177

Additional Sites	181
Kapilvastu	182
Lauriya Nandangarh	184
Nairanjana and Pragbodhi	185
Kaushambi	186
Kesariya	187
Hajipur	188
Gurpa	189
Vikramasila	189
Vaishali	190
Patna	194
Amravati	194
Ajanta Caves	196
Ellora Caves	196
Dhauli Hill	197
Nagarjuna Konda	198
Tso Pema	200
Dharamsala	204
Gyuto University	207
Palpung Sherabling	208
Boudhanath Stupa	210
Swayambunath Stupa	215
Notes	219
Glossary	227
Index	237

Venerable Choje Lama Karma Shedrup

Foreword

I am very grateful to *Namo Buddha Publications,* Palpung Institute, and Zhyisil Charitable Trust, for the publication of this book in which the great Kagyu master Khabje Khenchen Thrangu Rinpoche expounds not only the meaning of the different aspects of the Buddha's teachings, but also brings together and illuminates three special topics: the life and major deeds of the Buddha, the development of Buddhism, and pilgrimage to holy sites.

As the enlightened Buddha is the embodiment of dharmakaya, his very presence and every activity is a teaching and an example. As a Buddhist it is essential to have an awakened knowledge of the Buddha's life story in order to enter and follow the path of the true dharma.

After the Buddha's passing, his uncorrupted teachings and blessings continue to be of benefit to oneself and others to help to pacify negative karma, develop inner clarity and peace for spiritual growth.

At the time of Buddha Shakyamuni, he himself said that devotees should make pilgrimage to and pay homage at the main

Buddhist historical sites, blessed by past Buddhas and to be blessed by the Buddhas yet to come.

Through this we recollect and rejoice in the noble deeds and qualities of the Buddha which blesses us in order to help strengthen our practice to achieve the fruition of the sublime Dharma.

Therefore, through the unsurpassable understanding of the Buddha's life and deeds, the noble efforts of those to preserve the Dharma, and the merit of pilgrimage, I pray that all beings be inspired to enter and progress on the path of enlightenment.

Palpung Thubten Chokyi Ghatsal
Buddhist Institute
Auckland, New Zealand

2 December 2007

Chapter 1

THE LIFE OF THE BUDDHA

The story of how Buddhism developed begins, of course, with the story of Buddha Shakyamuni,[1] who is the guide for all Buddhists. We should not make the mistake of believing that since the Buddha was born in India he taught in a typically Indian style. The Buddha was born for a very special purpose: he came to this world in order to help and teach the whole of mankind, and also all other sentient beings, the path that leads to happiness.

Examining the main religions of the world, one will find that all the great teachers, whether Christian, Muslim or Buddhist, were very special people. They all had extremely pure motivation and aspiration to help other beings. When they came to teach other beings it wasn't in the way of a military conquest, but rather in the form of a teaching that was intended to help beings find happiness. So most of these great teachers gave teachings that remain even today, while military empires have come and gone by the hundreds. One may wonder why those teachings spread so widely, and why they are still around today. The reason is that these teachers had a very pure motivation to help others, from the very beginning. They taught true, pure paths that could lead to happiness.

The Buddha Shakyamuni's teachings have been practiced for 2,500 years and, considering the history of people who practiced Buddhism, we find that the teachings generated little suffering, problems or difficulties. On the contrary, a great number of people found peace and liberation through these teachings.

THE TWELVE DEEDS OF THE BUDDHA

There are many great deeds of the Buddha recorded, but these can be summarised under the twelve most important, most famous deeds.[2] The first of these twelve deeds occurred when the Buddha was teaching in the paradise of Tushita, which is in the *god realms*.[3] While the Buddha was teaching there, his previous motivation reminded him that it was necessary to take birth in Jambudvipa, and teach the dharma. He then considered five things: the land where he ought to be born, the caste he should be born into, the family in to which he should be born, who his mother was to be and that the time was right for him to be born (when the five degenerations were on the increase). After having made these determinations, he decided to leave Tushita paradise, and take birth in our world. This particular deed, of leaving Tushita to be born, had a special significance. It was intended to teach us that somebody who has achieved enlightenment is no longer constrained by *karma,* and has control over anything he or she does.

The second of the twelve great deeds of the Buddha was his entry into the womb of his mother, Mayadevi.[4] One may wonder why he took such a birth, if he had complete control over everything. Why wasn't he born miraculously from a lotus flower, as was Padmasambhava, or why didn't he simply descend from the sky? He didn't do this because, although it would have been very impressive and attracted many people, the Buddha was thinking of the long-term. His future disciples may have felt that it was all right for someone like the Buddha to practice and achieve enlightenment because he was a very special person from the beginning. They may have thought that ordinary human beings couldn't reach enlightenment because they didn't have these same miraculous powers. So the Buddha took a womb birth to show that even ordinary human beings can achieve the highest realisation; to instil conviction and confidence in his future disciples.[5]

The third special deed of the Buddha was his birth in the garden at Lumbini (which is in present day Nepal). Although the Buddha took an ordinary human birth there was still something very special about his birth. He came out of the body of his mother through her right side. Some people might start wondering how this was possible. They might think, "Well, what exactly happened? Did the rib cage crack?" One doesn't need to think in terms of anatomical problems because the Buddha was a miraculous being, and he just took birth through his mother's right side.

At the time of the Buddha's birth there were many very special things happening where he was born. Suddenly, some crops started growing. Trees appeared all over the area of Lumbini, and some very special flowers, such as the Udumbara flower that had never grown in this area, started blooming everywhere. From that moment onwards he was given the name of Siddhartha, in Sanskrit or Dundrup in Tibetan, which means "The One That Makes

Everything Possible." As a result of interdependent origination, the presence of a high being, especially his or her birth, produces changes in the environment, such as flowers blooming.[6]

A few years later, when the Buddha had grown up a little, he trained in all possible arts, crafts and sciences, and thus became very knowledgeable, very scholarly and very skilful. This was his fourth deed. This may be a little surprising because the Buddha was already enlightened, or at least a great *bodhisattva* residing on the tenth bodhisattva level (Skt. *bhumi*). It should not have been necessary for him to train in worldly skills because he should have known them naturally. However, there was again a specific reason for doing this, and this was to counteract various misconceptions which people might have had. One misunderstanding may be to think that the Buddha was someone who was simply a meditator, without any academic education. Another was the idea that he already possessed all this knowledge and didn't need to learn. This could give rise to the doubt that if ordinary humans tried to learn something it would lead to no results. So to overcome these misconceptions the Buddha worked at becoming a scholar and became very skilled in all different arts. It also shows that it is necessary to receive full education in the culture in which we are appearing. We must be fully at one with various positive aspects of our culture in order to become a vehicle for transmitting the dharma.

The fifth deed of the Buddha was to marry, have a child and enjoy the company of his queen, Yashodhara, as well as consorts and all the pleasures of royalty. He did this so that his future disciples wouldn't think that the Buddha, or an enlightened person, was unable to enjoy any pleasures. The other reason for living such a sensuous life was to show that, even though the Buddha had all the finest pleasures; it did not bring him satisfaction. He had understood that there was a higher form of happiness to be sought.

The sixth deed of the Buddha was his renunciation. The palace was enclosed with high walls and four gates: one facing each of the cardinal directions. The Buddha began to walk outside the precincts of the palace, each time leaving through a different gate. The first time he went out through the eastern gate of the palace he saw the suffering of an old man, and discovered for the first time that all people experience the degeneration of body. Another time he left the palace through the southern gate and, seeing a sick person, discovered the suffering that all people, at one time or another, experience. Next he went out through the western gate and, seeing a dead person, discovered the pain of death, which everyone must undergo. This hit him really hard because he realised that no matter how rich or powerful you are, and no matter how much pleasure and enjoyment you have, there is no way to escape from the suffering of old age, sickness, and death. No one can fight and defeat these three kinds of suffering.

Then the Buddha realised that maybe there is a way out, which is the practice of a spiritual path. The Buddha understood this when he left the palace through the northern gate and saw a monk. At this point he felt great weariness and renounced the world at the age of twenty-nine.[7]

His seventh deed was the practicing of austerities for six years, near the Nairanjana river in India. The austerities did not lead to his enlightenment, but these years were not wasted. They had a specific purpose of showing future disciples that the Buddha had put an enormous amount of effort, perseverance and diligence into realising the goal of enlightenment. This seventh deed was also to show that, as long as someone is attached to money, food, clothes and all the pleasures of life they can't really dedicate themselves to spiritual practice. However, if one gives up attachment then it is possible to achieve Buddhahood without too much difficulty. So that is why the Buddha engaged in six years of austerities by a riverside.

The eighth deed of the Buddha was his giving up of the austerities by accepting a bowl of yoghurt, going to the bodhi tree and vowing to stay there until he reached complete enlightenment. In contrast to the austerities, the Buddha ate nutritious food and gave his body a rest; he put his clothes back on and went to the bodhi tree. The Buddha gave up the austerities to show his future followers that the main object of Buddhist practice is working with one's mind. We have to eliminate the negativity in our mind, and develop the positive qualities of knowledge and understanding. True practice should be in the middle of the two extremes: practicing too many austerities, and being too indulgent. The first extreme is when you starve yourself, or you don't allow yourself food and drink. These practices also involve placing yourself in extreme physical conditions, such as being too hot or too cold. This is pointless because it has no true significance. The other extreme is where you just follow any of your desires. This is endless because there is a constant escalation of desires: if you have ten pleasures you'll want a hundred; if you have a hundred you'll want a thousand. You will never find any satisfaction, and you will also never be able to practice the dharma. So the Buddha wanted to show us that we have to avoid the extremes of too much austerity and too much indulgence: that practice lies somewhere in the middle.

The ninth deed of the Buddha is called "The subduing of the *mara,* Papiyan," with Papiyan being the leader of the Maras. This happened when the Buddha was sitting under the bodhi tree. Mara used forms related to the three *disturbing emotions* [Skt. *klesha*], of ignorance, desire and aggression, in order to lure the Buddha away from his pursuit of enlightenment.

The first deception, representing ignorance, was that the Buddha was asked to abandon his meditation and return immediately to the kingdom because his father, King Shuddhodana, had died, and the evil Devadatta had taken over the kingdom. This did not disturb the Buddha's meditation, so Mara then tried to create an obstacle using desire. He showed the Buddha his beautiful daughters, who tried to deceive and seduce him in all possible ways. When this did not disturb the Buddha's meditation, Mara then used hatred: coming towards the Buddha surrounded by countless horribly frightening warriors who were throwing weapons at the Buddha's body. But the Buddha wasn't distracted or fooled by these three poisons. He remained immersed in compassion and loving-kindness, and therefore triumphed over this display of the three poisons.

The tenth deed of the Buddha was his enlightenment, which he reached while meditating under the bodhi tree. Because the Buddha had developed all the qualities of meditation to the utmost he was able to reach enlightenment, which he did to show that we also have the same potential. As a matter of fact, the main point of the whole Buddhist philosophy is to show us that Buddhahood is not something to be found outside, but something we can achieve by looking inside ourselves; we can achieve enlightenment in the same way as the Buddha Shakyamuni reached enlightenment. The qualities that we will attain with enlightenment will be no different from the ones that the Buddha attained. We can also purify whatever negative emotions the Buddha managed to purify. The Buddha started as a bodhisattva, and then became someone who achieved enlightenment, to show us that we, also, can do the same.[8]

The eleventh deed of the Buddha occurred when he turned the wheel of the dharma three times, which means when he gave the three great cycles of teachings. At the time of the Buddha, the people of India believed that if one made offerings and prayed to a god then that god would be satisfied and happy, and in return would give you liberation and happiness. They also believed that if you didn't make offerings and pray to the gods they would be very angry, throw you down to the hells and inflict other states of suffering upon you. This idea of gods isn't really one of a special deity, they are only the embodiment of desire and aggression.

In Buddhism, we do not expect our happiness or our suffering to come from the Buddha. It is not believed that if we please the Buddha he will bring us happiness, and if we displease the Buddha he will throw us into some lower realm. The possibility of happiness or reaching liberation is entirely up to us. If we practice the path that leads to liberation we will attain Buddhahood, but if we do not practice it, then we cannot expect to reach enlightenment: it's in our hands whether we want to find happiness or suffering. But still, there is something that comes from the Buddha, and this is the path to liberation. To provide us with that means for liberation the Buddha turned the wheel of the dharma.

The twelfth deed of the Buddha was his passing away which was in the town of Kushinagar. He asked his students if they had any final questions, and then lying in the "lion's posture" he passed away. His last words were "Bhikshus, never forget, decay is inherent in all composite things."

Chapter 2

THE THREE WHEELS OF DHARMA

In the previous chapter the twelve deeds of the Buddha were discussed. The eleventh deed of the Buddha was turning the wheel of dharma. What is the actual meaning of this phrase? When we speak of dharma, we usually refer to the teachings given by the Buddha, but in fact dharma has two meanings: one is the scriptural dharma that came down to us from the Buddha and the other is the dharma of realization. Actually, the root of all dharma is realization, meaning that one understands the true nature of phenomena just as it is. To obtain such understanding, one has to develop all the good qualities of meditation with much diligence, effort, and perseverance. Through this work in meditation, one comes to a point where a special understanding, knowledge, and insight never experienced before arises. At this time one reaches the ultimate fruition, true realization. This is what is meant by the dharma of realization. But in order to achieve this realization, we need a foundation to work from. We need to work from the scriptural dharma which is the dharma as a teaching given us by the Buddha.

There are two main classes of scriptural dharma: the teachings of the sutras and the teachings of the *tantras*. The sutras of the Buddha were given in three different waves or turnings of the *wheel of dharma*. The first turning of the wheel of dharma was the *Hinayana* or Foundation vehicle teachings. These teachings were intended for individuals whose mind was not yet very open and who had a lesser aspiration to achieve enlightenment.

The second wave of teachings, called the second turning of the wheel of dharma, are the teachings on *emptiness* and the Prajnaparamita teachings. These are teachings of the *Mahayana*.

Finally, the third wave of teachings was the bridge between the sutras and the tantras. These were the teachings in which the Buddha taught that absolutely everyone has *Buddha nature* or Buddha essence.

THE SUTRAS

The first turning of teachings were given in Varanasi, which you can visit in India nowadays. The Buddha taught in the deer park (which is now called Sarnath), which at the time was a very remote and solitary place.[9] After the Buddha reached his enlightenment, he remained completely silent and didn't teach for seven weeks. The reason for this was to show that the dharma is very rare, special, valuable, and this is why the Buddha just remained silent for some time until he was requested to teach. The request was made by many gods including Brahma.[10] Having had the request to teach, the Buddha went to Varanasi and gave the teachings in the deer park. He gave the teachings to five men who were called "the five good followers,"[11] who were connected by previous karma to the Buddha and who through this link, were the first ones to receive his teaching.

The subject matter of this first turning of the wheel of dharma was the teaching of the *Four Noble Truths*. The Buddha expounded these Four Noble Truths to make it very clear to all those who were going to follow the Buddha's path what the teachings are, why one needed to practice it, and what kind of results one could be expected from the practice. So to clarify the path the Buddha laid it out in the very clear form of the four truths.

He showed that if we don't practice the path of dharma, we will wander on and on in samsara, but if we practice the dharma, we will gain the liberation of *nirvana*. The Buddha first taught that suffering is inherent to samsara and that this is what we must really overcome. Second, he taught that the cause of this suffering is the disturbing emotions or kleshas and karma. To counteract samsara we must engage in the aspect of nirvana, which again has two parts. The third noble truth of cessation or peace shows what we can achieve. Nirvana is cessation of suffering. And fourth, the way to achieve this is the truth of the path. Since samsara is by nature suffering, we have to go beyond samsara to eliminate samsara. Since nirvana is peace, this is what we have to try to achieve. But achieving nirvana and eliminating samsara cannot be done automatically. It is through working on the causes of these that we can achieve our goal. This is why the Buddha expounded on the four truths in the form of causes and their effects. The causes of the suffering of samsara are the disturbing emotions such as lust, anger, ignorance, and karma, which need to be overcome. In the same way, the cause of the peace and bliss of nirvana is the path, which needs to be practiced.

So this is how the Buddha gave the whole outline of his teaching in the form of these four truths. Within each aspect of samsara and nirvana, there is this causal relationship between cause and effect.

This series of teachings that began in Varanasi were called the turning of the first wheel of dharma. Later the Buddha turned the wheel of dharma for the second time at Vulture Peak in Rajgir, India.[12] The people who were present during this teaching were *arhats* and bodhisattvas in great numbers. The teaching itself was mostly the exposition of the Prajnaparamita. This is when the Buddha gave the teachings on emptiness and on the conduct of a bodhisattva through the teachings on the six *paramitas*.

In the first turning of the wheel of dharma, the Buddha showed that one had to abandon samsara to achieve nirvana. But how is this possible? Does it mean that we have to go on a long journey to where we have never been before to find nirvana? Does it mean that we have to create something new called nirvana? In fact, it doesn't mean that at all. All it means is that we have to understand the actual nature of phenomena,[13] we have to understand that our present view of reality is mistaken, and we have to remove our impurities. Once we see things as they really are, this is when we can achieve Buddhahood.

The third turning of the wheel of dharma is also called the teachings that gave complete clarification. These teachings were given in Shravasti and other places in India in the presence of all the great bodhisattvas. These teachings revealed that Buddha nature is present in the mind of all beings. We may wonder why this was taught last. The reason is that in the second turning, the Buddha taught that everything was empty of inherent nature. This teaching could lead to the belief that the goal of the Buddhist path—nirvana—is actually simply complete emptiness or annihilation.

To avoid this mistake, the Buddha gave this third set of teachings showing that the mind is not just nothingness. When one achieves Buddhahood, the original intrinsic luminosity of the mind becomes manifest. This luminosity or clarity of the mind means that the mind is not a dark, obscure thing by nature, but has its own inherent, intelligent clarity. Once one has removed the veils, the thick shroud of ignorance, the inherent clarity of the mind, this brilliance of the intelligence of mind, will shine in its fullness. Once this clarity of the mind has manifested, then one can understand all of nirvana and samsara very clearly. One has the understanding of phenomena and this knowledge is accompanied by the greatest bliss and peace.

THE TANTRAS

The three turnings of the wheel of dharma that have just been described correspond to the sutras taught by the Buddha. The Buddha also taught the tantras, which are the teachings of the *Vajrayana*. The Buddha gave four tantras: the *kriya tantras*, the *charya tantras*, the *yoga tantras*, and the *anuttarayoga tantras*.

These teachings were given in many places. Sometimes the Buddha gave these teachings in some of the god realms such as Tushita, and some of the teachings were given in physical places in India. Those receiving these teachings were bodhisattvas and *dakas* and *dakinis* practicing the *secret mantras*. The sutras already provided very deep and vast teachings on the nature of phenomena. But with the Vajrayana, the Buddha was able to give people the possibility of achieving the fruition of the Buddhist path very quickly and without major hardships. The Vajrayana can do this by providing special *skillful means* such as the meditation on the *generation stage* and the *completion stage* of a deity, and using meditation techniques of looking at the nature of the mind directly.

So the Buddha turned the wheel of dharma and gave all the various teachings of the Foundation vehicle, the Mahayana, and the Vajrayana[14] in different places with different people and at all different times. But also because he was teaching students of vastly different abilities, at times it seemed to them as if the Buddha was mainly spreading the Foundation vehicle; at times it seemed to them as if he was teaching the Mahayana and sometimes the Vajrayana. Of course, this was just a matter of the way in which the people were perceiving the teachings of the Buddha; it seemed to some that the Buddha was giving completely Foundation vehicle teachings and to others that he was giving completely Mahayana teachings. The Buddha could also be somewhere else and through his miraculous powers giving other teachings to others.

Because of this, some people started having the impression that the Buddha had only given the Foundation vehicle teachings, and had not given the Mahayana teachings which were made up by someone else. Others believed that the Buddha had given the Mahayana teachings, but had not given the Vajrayana teachings and that these Vajrayana teachings had been fabricated by his followers. The belief that the Mahayana and the Vajrayana teachings were created by someone else is based on the belief that the Buddha was just an ordinary man with no extraordinary qualities of enlightenment, instead of seeing a Buddha as being a very exceptional being who came into the world to help people out of his great compassion and to lead them to liberation. Once one thinks of the Buddha as an ordinary Indian man, then next one will have doubts as to whether he actually gave the various teachings attributed to him and one begins picking and choosing between teachings of the various vehicles.

It is a mistake to identify the Buddha as an ordinary person and to start thinking that maybe the Buddha didn't have complete knowledge, or was not able to teach a complete range of teachings, or that the Buddha could have taught in this place but not in that place. It is not worth entertaining such doubts because the Buddha was not an ordinary person nor was he a god who, if pleased with you, would send you to heaven and if displeased throw you into the hell realms. But at the same time, saying the Buddha is not a god doesn't mean that we should think of the Buddha as someone devoid of any special qualities of knowledge, intelligence and understanding or without any special direct intuition and insight. He was indeed a very special being who gave the complete set of dharma teachings, which were not in contradiction to each other. Each has its own relevance. Whoever practices a teaching of any level or vehicle properly will be able to achieve the respective result of that particular path. So this was the eleventh deed of the Buddha, the turning of the wheel of dharma.

The twelfth deed of the Buddha was his passing away.[15] The Buddha could have remained in our world for thousands and thousands of years, and this might have been quite beneficial. On the other hand, there would have been the danger that people would start thinking that the Buddha was permanent, which could generate all kinds of misconceptions. Instead by passing away, the Buddha showed that if he had to die, then, of course, everybody else would also have to die one day. So it was to make everyone aware of the impermanence of life, so that they could generate a sense of renunciation, a sense of urgency in their practice, a sense of weariness with this world. It was also to instill the feeling that dharma, the teachings of the Buddha, are very rare, precious and valuable. So this is why the Buddha passed away in Kushinagar in India.

Through his twelve deeds, the Buddha was able to help beings in our world extensively, particularly through the teachings of dharma. Why did the Buddha come into our world and act through these twelve deeds? The reason was the very exceptional compassion of the Buddha, wanting to help all beings and to lead them onto the path that leads to real happiness. He wanted to show individuals the path to peace, the path to true happiness by teaching the four truths or the two truths that describe the true nature of everything. He showed us that we have the choice to choose our own happiness and travel on the path that leads to ultimate liberation and happiness. So the Buddha, because of his very great love and compassion for all of us, did not keep these teachings to himself, but turned the wheel of dharma.

The First Council

After the Buddha passed away, his teachings were preserved without any alteration or without any loss by means of three great councils. The Buddha didn't speak from books that he had written and he didn't write anything down. Instead people came and asked him questions and voiced their doubts and their uncertainties. The Buddha would answer these questions, so that the teachings of the Buddha were actually answers to various people's questions and doubts. These questions would become the opportunity for expounding the truth, for speaking of the true nature of everything.

We may ask, "Well, if everything was just said by the Buddha and nothing was written down, how come things didn't get lost or altered or modified as time went on?" The reason this did not happen was that many of those who were receiving the Buddha's teaching were monks totally dedicated to the path of the Buddha.

When they listened to the teachings, they did it with all their heart and immediately put the teachings into practice so they realized the fruition of the path extremely quickly, allowing all the qualities of intelligence to rapidly blossom in them. Among other things, they achieved the power of perfect memory which means each word the Buddha said was engraved very deeply in their memory, so that every word was kept in their minds and nothing was lost.

After his passing away one of the Buddha's most important monks named Mahakashyapa gathered 500 arhats for a great council to keep all the teachings intact. The meeting took place in the great Sattapanni cave, which is quite close to Vulture Peak near Rajgir. So these 500 arhats gathered there and the meeting was presided over by three of them in particular: Ananda, Mahakashyapa, and Upali. They recited every word of the Buddha that they had heard and each of these three expounded on a particular aspect of the teachings of the Buddha: Upali expounded the Vinaya teachings, Ananda the Sutras, and Mahakashyapa the Abhidharma. They would begin by saying, "Thus have I heard. This is how the Buddha spoke," and then they would recite everything they had heard. In this way, they established very clearly and formally what the Buddha's teachings were, so from that point onwards all the teachings were classified into these three groups and kept very systematically.

The purpose of this first council was to make sure that all the immaculate words of the Buddha would be preserved in their purity and wouldn't be lost. For instance, if even one part of a sutra had been lost, then the whole teaching of the Buddha would have lost some of its meaning. That is why they wanted to keep everything intact. But, of course, it is possible that some of us will have doubts about this. We may feel that if there were no books to record the teachings of the Buddha, then maybe the sutras are not complete or maybe some of them have been made up by his followers, so it is quite possible that the sutras are not pure teachings at all.[16]

Well, we do not need to entertain that kind of doubt because the arhats were very great beings who respected the Buddha's teaching so deeply that they wanted to keep the teachings very pure: as they had been delivered originally by the Buddha.

Chapter 3

THE SECOND AND THIRD DHARMA COUNCILS

The first council was intended to make sure that all the teachings of the Buddha were kept intact and wouldn't be lost. This happened after the death of the Buddha and mainly consisted of gathering all the teachings together and keeping each category of teaching (the Sutras, Vinaya, and Abhidharma) very clear and very well defined. Each sutra was kept complete and each chapter was kept clearly separate so that nothing would get mixed up or altered. In this way, the first council established what the teachings of the Buddha really were and under which form they had been presented.

Later, the second council, sometimes called the intermediate council, took place 110 years after the Buddha had passed away (in the year 376 B.C.). At that time there had been a greater number of new monks joining the *sangha* and some of them started thinking that some of the rules of discipline laid out by the Buddha were too strict. They tried to establish another ten new rules.[17] They wanted to say that these new rules were actually made up by the Buddha. This second council had to be convened to make sure that the teachings wouldn't become modified because of these people's initiative.

To give an idea of the kind of things that these monks wanted to introduce, one was this, if you had done some negative action, then it would be sufficient to fold your hands to your heart and to say something like "hulu, hulu" and then it would be purified and you wouldn't need to do anything else. Another thing they wanted to introduce was that if a monk had done something wrong that went against the discipline of the monastery, then all he would need to say was, "I'm going to confess this." Another monk would say, "Oh, that's very good" and that would be enough and everything would be purified. So they were trying to introduce a lot of simplifications and easy ways of doing things.

During this time, there was a very exceptional being who was an arhat called Yashah. He saw this happening and realized that if nothing was done, the teachings of the Buddha would be altered and perverted. To prevent this from happening, he convened this second council with several other famous arhats.

Where did the trouble originate about these new monks trying to create new rules? At the time in India, there were six main cities, and the group of monks who wanted to start these new rules all came from Vaishali. So the arhat Yashah invited seven hundred arhats to meet for the council in Vaishali. He led the meeting by saying, "Well, now we have these ten new items that these monks are trying to introduce. The questions we should ask ourselves are whether these ten items can be found in the Sutras or in the Vinaya or in the Abhidharma." He asked all of the arhats that were present where these could be found and all of the arhats replied that they couldn't be found in any of these works. Then he asked, "Are these items in contradiction with the teachings of the Buddha; of the Sutras, the Vinaya, and the Abhidharma?" And the conclusion was that they were in contradiction with the words of the Buddha. As a result, they decided that these rules should be rejected because they didn't agree with what the Buddha had taught and certainly were not part of the teachings of the Buddha.

It was decided that this attempt to introduce new rules should be stopped and that these ten rules should be eliminated. Then the council took advantage of this situation to define once again very clearly what the teachings of the Buddha were so that there was a new, complete reading of the whole of the Sutras, the whole of the Vinaya, and the whole of the Abhidharma to make sure that these teachings were the only ones to be recognized as the Buddha's teaching.

After the second council, little by little the different communities of monks started to split up into different groups. So at first there were four different groups of *shravakas* and then this gradually evolved into eighteen different categories of shravakas, almost like different sects. Then each group started feeling that they really held the true teaching of the Buddha and their view was the right one and all the other groups were wrong. This, of course, generated a lot of arguments and debates creating a new danger that the teachings of the Buddha might be altered and degraded. So at this time a third council was convened.

The Third Council

At the third council there were 500 arhats led by the arya Parsva and there were also 400 venerables or scholars with the main one being Vasumitra. The meeting took place in the "land of the Moslems" and this is commonly used to refer to Kashmir. It took place there in a new temple (the Karnikavana Temple) that had been built especially for the occasion by the king.

The individuals meeting were of eighteen different sects of shravakas and the council had to determine which ones were really true followers of the Buddha and which were not. The guideline that was used to decide which were right and which were wrong was one of the sutras of the Buddha called the *Garland of Gold Sutra*. This sutra is a story concerning something that happened at the time of the previous Buddha, the one that came before Buddha Shakyamuni, Buddha Kashyapa. At the time of the Buddha Kashyapa, there was a king called Krikin, who had ten very amazing dreams. His dreams were so unusual that he started to wonder what was happening to him. And he thought that maybe these dreams were a sign that either there was going to be some very bad danger for his kingdom or even to his own life.

So he called in a Brahmin who was a specialist in the interpretation of dreams and asked him to say what he thought of the dreams. The Brahmin said that indeed, there was going to be a lot of trouble for the kingdom and a danger for his own life if he didn't kill the closest thing to his heart.

The closest thing to his own heart was his daughter who was called "Garland of Gold," and she was a Buddhist and didn't like the Brahmins. So once the king had heard the interpretation of his dream, his daughter said to him, "Well, it's very easy. What you should do is to go see the Buddha Kashyapa, and ask him if he thinks it's the right thing to kill me. Then, please go ahead. I don't mind."

So the king went to see Buddha Kashyapa and told him about his dreams, and Buddha Kashyapa replied that the dreams didn't mean that there would be any trouble for the king himself or his kingdom. The dreams were, in fact, foreseeing events that would happen much later on in a future time. He said each of the dreams depicted events that would take place at the time of Buddha Shakyamuni. So each of the dreams referred to an event in Buddhism with one being applicable to the situation at the time of the third council. In this dream the king saw a long piece of cloth and there were eighteen men who were each trying to get a piece of the cloth. In the end each one got a piece and there were eighteen pieces of cloth.

The Buddha Kashyapa interpreted this as, "This dream hasn't anything to do with your own life as the king. But at the time of Buddha Shakyamuni, there will be eighteen different schools of shravakas. But one shouldn't think that their views are in contradiction with the teachings of Buddha Shakyamuni. In fact, the whole of Buddha Shakyamuni's teachings remains pure and intact, and each of the paths that they are following is the true path and leads to the true fruition. So one mustn't think that some are good and some are bad. Each of the paths belongs to the true path of the Buddha."

So this was the prophesy made by Buddha Kashyapa in the sutra. And that is why the council had to come to the conclusion that each of these eighteen sections of shravakas were all correct in their line of thought and that the teachings that they were following were all the teachings of Buddha Shakyamuni.

During this third council, they also completed their previous work on the gathering of the Vinaya, the Sutras, and the Abhidharma. During the previous councils, they had started to write down these three sections of the Buddha's teachings. By the third council some of these works were already written down. So during the third council they corrected the proofs of what had been written down, so that these teachings were now pure and could be decisively considered as the Buddha's teaching. Then they finished writing down those teachings that were yet not written down. We can say that after the third council was over, all of the Buddha's teachings were finally written down and corrected; so from that point onwards there could be no distortion, no misinterpretation or any alteration of the Buddha's true teachings. This was the work of all these very learned arhats who had a great deal of spiritual insight and a very clear understanding. So through their work the whole of the Buddha's teaching was preserved without loss, without distortion, and remained completely intact.

Chapter 4

THE MAHAYANA AND VAJRAYANA COUNCILS

This *history of the three councils* actually relates more directly to the way in which the Foundation vehicle teachings were preserved, particularly, the Foundation vehicle tradition of the Vinaya. But a similar thing happened in the Mahayana tradition. Some time after the passing away of the Buddha one million bodhisattvas met together under the leadership of the three great bodhisattvas, Vajrapani, Maitreya, and Manjushri on the top of mount Vimalasvabhava, which lies south of Rajgir in northern India. All the teachings of the Buddha were also collected in the three same sections of Sutras, Vinaya, and Abhidharma. The bodhisattva Vajrapani recited the Sutras, the bodhisattva Maitreya recited the Vinaya, and the bodhisattva Manjushri recited the Abhidharma. So in this meeting they also collected all the teachings of the Buddha and classified them into these three main categories.

A similar thing took place with the Vajrayana teachings. The Buddha taught four categories of tantras: the kriya tantra, the charya tantra, yoga tantra, and anuttarayoga tantra. With the lower three tantras (that is, the kriya tantra, charya tantra and yoga tantras) there was a special meeting of all the bodhisattvas in the god realm to gather all of these teachings, led by Vajrapani. For this reason, in the Vajrayana tradition he is known as "the Lord of Secrets," with secrets referring to the secret mantra, that is, the Vajrayana. How did he come to be the Lord of Secrets? First he was the one who requested the Buddha to turn the profound dharma wheel of the tantras and then, when it was turned, he was the most prominent of the disciples. Later when there was this meeting of the bodhisattvas to collect all the lower tantras, Vajrapani was the leader of this gathering and it is through his action that the tantras have been preserved up to now.

As far as the anuttarayoga tantras were concerned, the *father tantras* and *mother tantras* were mostly requested and received by dakinis such as Vajrayogini, and it was also the wisdom dakinis who collected and preserved these teachings. The *Hevajra Tantra* was transmitted mostly to the bodhisattva Vajragarbha. He later on gathered the teachings and transmitted them in their integrity.

The *Kalachakra Tantra* was transmitted mostly to the Dharma King Sucandra. He was actually an emanation of Manjushri. He was the one who also kept the teachings, collected them, and passed them on.

The Shastras

All the different categories of the Buddha's teaching including the sutras and the tantras were transmitted to disciples who didn't just hear these teachings, but who practiced and preserved them so that they were transmitted all the way down to the present time without any defect, alteration or loss.

There are two main categories of the dharma. First there are the actual teachings of the Buddha, and then there are the *shastras*, which are the works that elucidate the meaning of the Buddha's teachings. We've heard about the twelve deeds of the Buddha, and about the three councils and how these allowed all the actual teachings of the Buddha to remain intact and faultless up to now. As Buddhism developed and spread in India, many different scholars wrote works trying to elucidate and clarify the meaning of the Buddha's teachings for others. So these works are what we call the shastras.

The shastras are intended to make the original teaching of the Buddha easier to understand. They do not contain any personal ideas of the writer and do not put forward the author's own theory about anything. So when a teaching of the Buddha is very long and very detailed, the shastras present a summarized, easier to understand form of these teachings. Then when a teaching of the Buddha is rather complex, the shastras make these teachings much more easily understandable. Finally, when a teaching of the Buddha on a particular topic is scattered in many different sutras, then a shastra may take all these different points concerning the same subject and collect them in one place. So the importance of the shastras is to present the meaning of the Buddha's teaching in a form that is easy for people to understand. One could say that the meaning of these shastras is so close to the Buddha's teaching that it could almost be counted as being part of the actual teachings of the Buddha.

Some people have doubts because they think that maybe the shastras were just concoctions by different writers and scholars that don't really have anything to do with the Buddha's teachings. They also make too much distinction between what is in the scriptures of the Buddha and what is in the shastras. But one shouldn't think that there is a great difference between what the Buddha taught and the shastras, the meditation instructions and the *spiritual songs*. They should be thought of as a whole, as the same teachings that originated from what the Buddha taught. So whether dealing with the actual words of the Buddha or the instructions of realized masters, we should consider them all as having the same value. Whether we practice the teachings given by the Buddha or the teachings laid out in the shastras, there is no difference except that maybe we will find the shastras a little easier to understand. This is why Tibetans favored the shastras so much.

The Buddha taught the various levels of the dharma by giving teachings of the Foundation vehicle, the Mahayana and the Vajrayana. It is said in a sutra of the Buddha that whenever the Buddha speaks even one word, that word can be heard in different places, in different times, in different ways by the various people according to their spiritual maturity. This means that when the Buddha was teaching, those who were ready for the Foundation vehicle received his teaching from the Foundation vehicle viewpoint and accordingly were able to practice this path and achieve the Foundation vehicle fruition. Simultaneously, someone who was ready for the Mahayana received the teaching from the Mahayana point of view and through practicing this was able to achieve the Mahayana fruition. The same applies also to the Vajrayana.

In the Foundation vehicle tradition it is the Buddha's teachings that are most important. But in Tibet, the shastras became extremely important. One might think that this was rather strange because these shastras in Tibet became even more important in a way than the actual words of the Buddha. But this shouldn't lead us to think that the Buddha's teachings were forgotten, put aside and replaced by the shastras that were just fabricated by scholars who lived after the Buddha. In fact, what happened was that some individuals practiced the Buddha's teaching. They assimilated the meaning of his teachings so well that through the power and blessing of the teaching, they managed to achieve the fruition of the path; so that if they practiced the shravaka aspect of the path, they became arhats. If they practiced the Mahayana, they achieved the bodhisattva levels from the first up to the tenth bodhisattva level. Or if they practiced the Vajrayana, they achieved the ordinary and the supreme spiritual accomplishments, in particular, the power of direct, intuitive knowledge. Once they had achieved this fruition of the path they were then able to write a shastra which is a landmark, a guidebook for others who were to follow, to show them that if they understood the Buddha's teaching very well and practiced properly, this is what would happen, this is how one could go about it, this is how one should understand it, and so on. So the shastras that they wrote were not a contradiction of the Buddha's teaching, but a reinforcement of the Buddha's teaching.

Those scholars or *panditas* who wrote the shastras didn't necessarily write from their realization. If they wrote from their experience, the result was the same as teachings of the Buddha because they were so completely penetrated with the meaning of the Buddha's teaching and had assimilated it so perfectly that whatever they wrote was out of total conviction in the validity of the Buddha's teaching. Whatever they wrote wasn't just their own ideas put down on paper, but it was to make the Buddha's teaching more easily understandable to most people. This is why we should consider the shastras as being the same as the Buddha's teaching, not as being something foreign to the teaching.

THE THREE VEHICLES

Historically there were different ways each of these levels of the Buddha's teachings spread, according to the various degrees of spiritual maturity and readiness of people. There was a time in India when the Buddhist practices were mostly Foundation vehicle practice. It was the time of the seven patriarchs[18] and other great shravakas. Later on there was a great flourishing of the Mahayana teachings. This was at the time of the great University of Nalanda,[19] which had such great teachers as Nagarjuna and Asanga. Then still later on there was a great flourishing of the Vajrayana at the time when the University of Vikramashila was prominent with Tilopa, Naropa, and the other eighty-four *mahasiddhas*[20] living in India.

We will look at these three aspects of the Foundation vehicle, the Mahayana, and the Vajrayana in more detail in the following chapters.

Chapter 5
THE FOUNDATION VEHICLE PATH

When Buddhism first spread the seven great patriarchs emerged and due to them it was the dharma of the shravakas that became widely propagated. We call this path the "Hinayana" which literally means the "lower (or lesser) vehicle." But, of course, this is only a name and we shouldn't think that the Hinayana is an inferior vehicle of the Buddha's teaching. It was only that the Buddha was very skillful in his way of teaching people by giving them many ways to reach enlightenment, and the Hinayana or Foundation vehicle was one of these ways to come to the path and eventually reach liberation. So for a particular type of disciple, this type of teaching is best.

The Mahayana path emphasizes a very vast motivation. The Vajrayana emphasizes a very fast path that uses many different means to achieve the goal of enlightenment. This, however, does not mean that there was no need for teaching the Foundation vehicle, because the Buddha was able to help countless beings to enter the path of liberation and achieve the ultimate fruition in this way. The Foundation vehicle had this special capacity and therefore it was the content of the first turning of the wheel of dharma, and it was this aspect of the Buddhist teachings that developed and spread in India first, benefiting many people.

The gradual approach to the path of liberation is most important, and that is why the Buddha first taught the Hinayana or Foundation vehicle. The same thing is true of our own individual practice. We need the foundation of the Hinayana for all of our practice. In other words, we need to thoroughly think about karma, the inevitable link between our actions and their consequences. We also need to generate a very strong sense of renunciation of samsara. So we need to understand and to have developed all these things in ourselves before we can carry on practicing the other levels of the path. Someone who is a beginner cannot be expected to receive an immediate understanding of the deepest nature of phenomena and be ready to understand the ultimate truth. A good analogy is to look at the Buddhist path as a staircase. If you want to go to the top of a house, you need to go up the stairs one step after the other. If you try to jump from the bottom to the top, you will fall down and break your leg. But if you go up steadily and gradually, then your purpose will be very firm and stable. The same thing is true of dharma; you need the firm basis of the Hinayana to progress properly to the rest of the levels of the practice.

There is a very good example to illustrate this gradual approach. Milarepa in the beginning of his search for dharma was looking for a teacher who would give him a very profound teaching that could free him from all his bad deeds. He went to central Tibet in the provinces of U and Tsang. There he asked someone where he could find a very good lama who could give him very profound teachings. He was directed towards a great lama who used to give the teachings of the "great perfection" or *Dzogchen* teachings. Milarepa went to see this lama and he said, "I am a very great sinner and I need a teaching that will enable me to become a Buddha in this lifetime."

The lama replied, "Well, don't you worry, I've got just the teaching for you. I've got a very profound teaching, the Dzogchen teachings. If you meditate on it in the morning, in that very morning, you can become a Buddha. If you meditate at night, then that very same evening, you can become a Buddha. If you are a very special person who is spiritually mature with the right karma, then you don't even need to meditate. You will become enlightened immediately. So don't you worry. It will probably help you."

So Milarepa thought to himself, "Well, I must be one of those special people. I am spiritually mature and will develop realization very quickly." And then he went to meditate. And after some days, the lama came and said, "How are you getting on? Are you getting this sign or that sign or indication of progress in meditation?" But Milarepa had to admit that he had no signs whatsoever. Then the lama said, "Well, I'm afraid it must be as you said. You must be a really bad sinner. I don't think you can manage to become a Buddha. I think you'd better go and see somebody else. You should go and see the king of translators, Marpa. I think he will be able to help you."

So the lesson we can learn from this story is not that Milarepa was a poor meditator or that the Dzogchen teachings are bad. Milarepa was indeed a very special person and the Dzogchen teachings are especially profound. But someone who tries to begin with the deepest teaching won't receive very much benefit from them because one needs some preparation before going on to higher teachings. This is also the reason why the Buddha began his teachings with the Hinayana. This also shows us that the gradual approach in practice is the best. So we shouldn't consider that the Hinayana is a lower teaching. It is instead a very special and necessary level of the teaching.

The Hinayana of Foundation vehicle teachings were entrusted from teacher to disciple. First the Buddha entrusted them to his own disciple the shravaka Mahakashyapa. During his lifetime the Buddha made it very clear that he considered Mahakashyapa as his representative, empowering him thus and allowing him to sit on a throne half the height of his own. When the Buddha had passed away, it was Mahakashyapa who organized the first council with the 500 arhats. And after this council, Kashyapa himself passed away. Then his successor was another great disciple of the Buddha called arya Ananda who become the chief holder of the Foundation vehicle teachings after the passing away of Kashyapa. Then when Ananda died, he was succeeded by his own disciple named Upagupta who had great miraculous powers.

One example of Upagupta's powers is as follows: One time when he wanted to give teachings the mara Papiyan did not like this and emanated invisible devil-like dancers who would dance at the place of the teachings. So on the first day tens of thousands of people attended. On the second day the number of people receiving the teaching diminished, on the third day still fewer came and so on. Upagupta began to realize that there must be some obstacle to the teachings and when he examined this, he understood that it was due to the emanations of the mara Papiyan who managed to get the people to stay away from the teachings. On the seventh day Upagupta himself went to the dancing place through his miraculous powers and put a necklace of flowers around the neck of each of the dancing demons. But as soon as he had finished distributing the flower garlands, they changed into human and dog corpses. However much Papiyan tried to get rid of these, he could not liberate himself from them. In the end he had to go up to Upagupta and ask him to help remove them.

And Upagupta said, "Well if you can promise to stop interrupting the teachings, then I will remove these corpses for you." As he promised to create no more obstacles to the listening of the dharma, Upagupta took away the corpses. And after that, Papiyan admitted that really he had never seen anybody with such great miraculous powers. He said that in the past he did create many disturbances for the Buddha, but that he had never encountered such an amazing reaction from him. And then Papiyan asked Upagupta, "Did you ever meet the Buddha?" Upagupta replied, "I didn't meet his physical body, but I met his mind, the *dharmakaya*." He could say this because he was a realized shravaka arhat, and so the mara said, "Can you show me the Buddha?" And Upagupta was able to make an emanation of the Buddha, and although it wasn't a perfect copy of the Buddha, it was so similar that the mara was completely overwhelmed as he recognized the form of the Buddha. He then felt very strong faith towards this teacher and started prostrating to him. But the teacher said, "Please stop," and prevented him from doing the prostrations. He said, "If you do this, then my merits, my abilities and my powers will diminish." So he didn't want him to offer him prostrations.

This is just an example of the way in which Upagupta subdued the mara Papiyan. He was a very powerful teacher and with his teachings a lot of his disciples were able to become arhats. Under his guidance there were one or two people reaching arhatship every day. Every time someone became an arhat Upagupta would take a little square piece of wood and he would put it away in a cave. In the end, so many people had become arhats that the whole cave was filled up with these little wooden sticks.

At the time of the Buddha the followers of the Buddha relied entirely on the teachings of the Buddha, everything he had been telling them during his lifetime. Then at the time of the arhat Upagupta many other people achieved arhatship, and these arhats started a new tradition which was the tradition of writing commentaries on the Buddha's teachings. What they did was to gather together all the teachings of the Buddha and extract the essential meaning of all his teachings. Having done this, they wrote it out in this new kind of work called a shastra, or a teaching which is an explanation and elucidation of the Buddha's teachings. The first shastra was a work called the *Vibhasakosha* or *The Treasure of Special Explanations.* It was like a treasure because it contained all the meanings of the Buddha's teachings gathered into one, and it was a special explanation, because it explained them one by one anew. This work started a tradition of writing shastras which flourished later on.

We have mentioned the three great teachers Mahakashyapa, Ananda and Upagupta, who were three of the "seven patriarchs of the teachings." Most of these seven lived in Varanasi, where a great temple had been built and numerous members of the sangha had gathered. One might wonder if the teachings declined after these seven patriarchs had passed away. The transmission of the Foundation vehicle lineage was no longer passed onto one person alone, but was transmitted to many lineage holders. After the passing of the seven patriarchs we can no longer talk of single patriarchs, but only of transmission lineages.

The teaching transmissions were not interrupted, and this holds true for both the sutra and mantra teachings. In time, it spread from Varanasi to the monastic universities of Nalanda and

Vikramashila. My particular lineage, that of the Kagyu Buddhist school, received transmissions from the seven patriarchs through the *mahapandita* Naropa, who was abbot of Nalanda and received both the sutra and tantric lineages from this great university. Naropa passed the tantric lineage to Marpa who brought it from India to Tibet. Marpa passed it to his great student Milarepa, who had a student Gampopa, who had the first Karmapa as a student, and he founded the Karma Kagyu lineage. The sutra tradition passed on to Atisha, who was abbot of Nalanda university and Gampopa received this transmission of the sutras. So Gampopa received the sutra tradition of Atisha and the tantra tradition of Marpa. Thus Gampopa received the tradition of both the sutras and tantras, so that this very old tradition of the shravakas going back to Kashyapa is still alive in the Kagyu tradition.

Chapter 6

THE MAHAYANA PATH

Previously we saw how the teachings of the Foundation vehicle spread in India from Varanasi and how with the seven patriarchs the Foundation vehicle teachings emerged. Then as time went on, those who were spiritually inclined towards the Hinayana became less numerous. Gradually India entered a period of time when there was a new group of people who were especially suited for the Mahayana teachings and a great wave of propagation of the Mahayana teachings took place.

The main geographical point where the propagation of the Mahayana took place was the monastic University of Nalanda. There were many very great and learned masters or panditas at Nalanda University who expounded certain sutras such as the Mahayana *Lankavatara Sutra*. These panditas gradually developed logical arguments that all inner phenomena—thoughts, feelings, perceptions—were empty. In other words they developed the philosophical view of *Chittamatra*, the Mind-only school. Then gradually they established the view that outer phenomena such as trees and houses and mountains were also empty. In other words they developed the *Madhyamaka* (Middle-way) view.

The sutras and shastras that expound the Chittamatra view explained that the source of all our suffering, of all our problems, originates in a misconception or a delusion of what reality really is, and that this misunderstanding can be removed through understanding the actual nature of phenomena. When one sees the true nature of things, then the misunderstanding, the delusion, automatically disappears of its own accord. From the beginning of the Chittamatra school all the way up to the highest levels of the Vajrayana and the Mahamudra of today, instructions are given to remove one's misconception of the actual nature of things. This is the major intention of the Mahayana teachings. In contrast, the approach of the Foundation vehicle is to analyze and counteract the disturbing emotions such as anger and desire, which are the temporary cause of suffering. The practice of the Foundation vehicle, which results in pacifying these disturbing emotions, creates a temporary liberation. The idea of the Mahayana is to understand the nature of phenomena just as they are, and this will provide a more permanent liberation.

The Chittamatra School

The main idea of the Chittamatrins is that all outer manifestations such as mountains and houses arise from the mind. This is rather hard to believe for a beginner because it seems to us that everything outside of us is really there and we can't see how it could ever come from our mind. But if we examine this more closely, we will find that the Chittamatrins are right. We just need to take the example of a dream to understand how this works. If we are dreaming and suddenly a tiger appears in front of us, seeing that tiger will create fear. So this vision of the tiger will generate fear in our mind because we take the vision as an external thing. But in a dream there is no real tiger there in the first place. So what takes place is reversed. It isn't something outside that creates something in our mind, but rather our mind creates something perceived as being outside of us. So in our dream, our mind creates the appearance of the tiger and then we react to this appearance.

If we transpose this situation onto our ordinary waking life in samsara, everything we experience in the world, all these outer manifestations that surround us, seem to determine our state of mind so that whatever we experience as pleasant or unpleasant, we believe is due to what is happening outside us. But really, it's the other way around. Whatever appears to us does so because it comes from our mind. This then is presented in great detail by the Chittamatra school: the root of everything is in the mind and our mind determines everything we experience.

The Madhyamaka School

The main philosophy of the Mahayana is the Madhyamaka view. This Madhyamaka view was expounded by the Buddha in the sutras in the second and third turning of the wheel of dharma. There are accordingly two forms of Madhyamaka called "empty of self" (Tib. *Rangtong*) emphasizing the second turning of the wheel and "empty of other" (Tib. *Shentong*) emphasizing the third turning of the wheel.

The propagation of the Madhyamaka teachings took place in India at Nalanda University. One of the great masters at Nalanda was Nagarjuna. The Buddha had predicted the coming of Nagarjuna in the *Lankavatara Sutra*. The Buddha said that in the future in southern India in a place called Vedali, there would come a monk named Shrinat and sometimes he would also have the name of Naga. It also said his task would be to eliminate all biases of existence or non-existence and to establish the middle way of emptiness. So Nagarjuna would teach the Mahayana and in his lifetime he would achieve the first bodhisattva level called "the joyous one," and after his death, he would go to Dewachen, the land of great peace, great happiness. So according to this prediction of the Buddha, this is exactly what happened and Nagarjuna entered our world, took birth there, and everything happened as had been predicted.

Nagarjuna

The Buddha gave the teaching on emptiness in a work called the *Prajnaparamita* sutras. The longest form of the Prajnaparamita sutra consists of one hundred million shlokas. A shloka is a set of verses. Another long form is a sutra in ten million shlokas. But he did not propagate these very much. The ones that mainly spread were, in the longest form, the sutra in 100,000 shlokas. Then there is a slightly shorter form which is a sutra in 25,000 shlokas, and an even shorter one yet, 8,000 shlokas. Then there is a very concise form, called the *Sancayagatha*. Finally there is the mantra OM GATE GATE PARAGATE PARASAMGATE BODHI SVAHA, which summarizes the whole meaning of the Prajnaparamita in just a few syllables.

So these were the Prajnaparamita sutras, which Nagarjuna and his followers propagated and explained. In particular, he composed the Madhyamaka shastras, whose particular approach was to establish the validity of the view of emptiness expressed in the Prajnaparamita sutras by means of logic.

Nagarjuna's Followers

Nagarjuna had a lot of followers, disciples who propagated the teachings of the Buddha. Among these were Aryadeva, Dharmakirti and Shantideva. And at the time, there were not just Buddhists in India but also non-Buddhists, which in Buddhist terminology are called tirthikas. In those days they used to have very large debates of logic where they would try to outwit each other to prove the correctness and the validity of their own teachings. So they had many of these debates. The followers of Nagarjuna, particularly Aryadeva, were very skillful and through faultless logic managed to defeat all their opponents and establish the validity of the Buddha's teaching.

One example was Matriceta,[21] a famous tirthika scholar. He was extremely skilled at debates, very clever and skillful. He wasn't just a scholar, but had realized the deity of his own faith, he had realized the powers of Mahashvara. So his fame was great and most people were quite frightened at the prospect of having to debate with such a man, because he was very accomplished. This Matriceta arrived at Nalanda and he said, "I have come to challenge you to a debate. If there is anybody here who would like to debate with me, then we will do that. That's fine. But if nobody steps forward, then your whole university will have to be converted to my faith." So everybody was in a state of panic because nobody felt they could challenge Matriceta. So nobody wanted to step forward and debate with him.

The scholars of Nalanda knew they would never outwit Matriceta, so they prayed to *Mahakala* and asked him to send someone who would be able to help. They believed the only person who could get them out of this difficult spot was Nagarjuna, who at the time was residing at a mountain in southern India called Sri Parvata. They asked Mahakala to give a message to Nagarjuna and then they waited there praying and praying every day hoping that Nagarjuna would turn up for the debate. In the meantime Matriceta was just sitting there and counting the people and saying, "One cow, two cows, three cows." He thought they were so stupid that he called them cows. "That's one, and that's two and that's three," because they were just praying and waiting for Nagarjuna to turn up.

Nagarjuna didn't come himself but sent his disciple Aryadeva. But when he came using his miraculous powers, Aryadeva met with some difficulties. One of these was that someone begged him for his eye, and in response he gave his right eye. So he ended up without one of his eyes, so that when he arrived at Nalanda, he had only one eye left. On that day Matriceta was still counting the people and saying, "One cow, two cows, three cows." He saw Aryadeva coming and said, "Ah! And one eyeless cow." Then Aryadeva replied, "Well, Indra has one thousand eyes and he cannot see the nature of all phenomena, and your Mahashvara has three eyes, but he cannot see the nature of all phenomena. I may have just one eye, but I can see the true nature of phenomena." Then he accepted the debate with Matriceta.

Aryadeva said, "I will challenge you in a debate tomorrow morning. So come and bring all the things you want for the debate and I'll meet you in the morning." Then Aryadeva went to pray to Manjushri, and he asked Manjushri to advise him on what he should take to the debate. And Manjushri said, "You take one bottle of oil, a cat, and a dirty old shoe." Then on the day of the debate above Matriceta's seat was a very beautiful white parasol and Aryadeva tied the old shoe to the white umbrella so that it was just hanging over the head of Matriceta. Matriceta had also brought a few things including a very bright, clear mirror in which various things would appear for him and a parrot that would tell him many things.

They started debating. While they were talking, Matriceta would sometimes start looking into his mirror to get answers and ideas. Then Aryadeva poured the oil over the mirror so that Matriceta couldn't see anything in the mirror any more. At another point Matriceta got really stuck, so he started to get the parrot to give the answer. Then Aryadeva let the cat loose so that the cat neutralized the parrot. After the cat had neutralized the parrot, Matriceta saw that he was losing and he started calling out to his god, Mahashvara for help. But when Mahashvara started to come down, he saw the horrible old shoe dangling from the white umbrella on top of Matriceta's head, and thought that was really disgusting, so he didn't come down. So now Matriceta was left all to himself and was completely powerless. Then they just had to carry on the debate by normal means and Matriceta lost the contest. From that day onwards, there was no more trouble and the Buddhists were always able to use logic to defeat their opponents in debate. This is how the view of Madhyamaka spread, which is the interpretation of the second turning of the wheel of dharma. These teachings spread from the University of Nalanda to the rest of India and even beyond the borders of India.

The Story of Asanga[22]

After that came the time when the teachings of the third turning of the wheel of dharma spread in India. This was mainly the work of Asanga and some others. In the fourth century C.E. there was a tirthika greatly opposed to Nalanda and the monks of Nalanda. This man used his magical powers to cast a spell on Nalanda so that it caught fire. In the fire, the great library of Nalanda was burned, so that most of the Abhidharma teachings, both sutras and shastras, were burned. It became likely that most of the Abhidharma teachings would vanish unless something could be done. During this time there was a female bodhisattva who was a nun called Prasannashila. She realized what was happening and just couldn't bear the thought of all those very precious teachings of the Buddha being lost. She decided to do something to preserve the Abhidharma. She felt that she was too old to master the Abhidharma and spread it herself, so she left the order as a nun and had a relationship with a member of the royal family. From that union was born Asanga.

She then had another relationship with a Brahmin and from this union was born Vasubhandu. In India there was a tradition that whatever trade your father was in, you had to follow the same trade. So when the children had grown up somewhat, they started asking their mother questions about their fathers. They asked, "What did our father do? What was his occupation so we can do the same?" But their mother said to them, "I didn't give birth to you so that you would follow in the footsteps of your fathers. I conceived you because I realized that the Abhidharma teachings of the Buddha were going to be lost and I wanted both of you to do everything you could to preserve this teaching and spread it again. So this is now the task that you should set for yourselves."

The youngest son, Vasubhandu, was sent to Kashmir and there he studied the Abhidharma from the master Sanghabhadra and mastered the Abhidharma.

Asanga, the older brother, followed the path that had been given by his mother, which was to do the practice of Maitreya. In fact, Asanga's accomplishments had already been predicted by the Buddha in the *Manjushri Mula Tantra* in which the Buddha said that 900 years after his passing there would come a monk called Asanga who would be extremely skilled at writing shastras. This monk would be able to clarify all of the Buddha's teachings, expound them and explain them very clearly in terms of the absolute and the relative meaning. So through this monk the teachings would be explained in all their clarity.

Asanga practiced the *sadhana* of Maitreya for three years in a retreat and did not get any signs of accomplishment. He thought that he should abandon his practice, but when he left his cave, he encountered a man who was rubbing a large iron bar with a cotton cloth. Asanga asked him why he was doing this and the man replied that if he kept rubbing it more and more, he would be able to make a needle out of it. Asanga thought, "This person is doing all this work to get such an insignificant thing as a needle, and I am trying to accomplish something important, so I shouldn't get discouraged," and he returned to his cave. He practiced another six years and nothing happened, so he thought there was no point in carrying on. Then again he encountered a man who was rubbing with a feather a large boulder that was blocking the sunlight from his house. Asanga thought that if he is doing all this for just some sunlight, then practicing for nine years is nothing. So he returned and carried on another three years.

After a total of twelve years of meditation he had not attained anything, so he decided that he would never be able to accomplish something with this Maitreya practice, and finally gave it up and came out of his cave. When he was walking, he came across a dog the back half of which was rotting and full of maggots. When the dog saw Asanga, it began barking and wanted to bite him. Asanga was overwhelmed by all the suffering of the dog and all this negativity in the dog. Asanga wanted to help the dog, but realized that if he pulled the maggots out then the maggots would die, but that if he left these worms in, then the dog would die. Eventually he cut some flesh off his own leg to put the maggots on, but realized that if he pulled the maggots out with his fingers, that would kill them. So he decided to draw them out with his tongue, but he couldn't bear to look at what he was doing. So he closed his eyes and lifted out the maggots with his tongue, and put them on the piece of flesh. Then, the second time he stuck out his tongue, his tongue didn't touch the dog but touched the ground. So he opened his eyes and there was no a dog before him. Instead Maitreya was standing before him. When he saw Maitreya he became very upset and said, "Why do you have so little compassion? I have been practicing all these years and you never showed yourself to me." Maitreya replied, "It is not that I didn't have compassion for you, it is that you had too many obscurations and that is why you couldn't see me. But after practicing for twelve years, your obscurations became much less, so that you were able to see me in the form of a dog. Due to your compassion for this dog and your act of generosity in cutting off your own flesh and so on, you were then able to see me. If you don't believe me, I will sit on your shoulder and you will find out if others can see me." So Asanga did that and went into town to ask, "Is there anything on my shoulder?" Everyone said there was nothing there, except one old lady who said that he had a dog on his shoulder and wanted to know why he was carrying a dog around.

Asanga was convinced, and then he went to Tushita pure realm, where he stayed with Maitreya and received the five teachings of Maitreya. Maitreya taught on the Prajnaparamita in the *Abhisamayalankara Sutra*. He commented on the same Prajnaparamita sutras of the second turning of the wheel that Nagarjuna had commented on, but in a different way. Nagarjuna had emphasized the direct meaning of these sutras, that is, the emptiness of all phenomena. In contrast, Maitreya made what is indirectly taught in the Prajnaparamita explicit through the teachings on the bodhisattva paths covering what is attained and what is eliminated on the first level, what is attained and eliminated on the second level and so on.

In the third turning of the wheel of dharma there are the provisional teachings of the Chittamatra school view and the definitive teachings of Buddha nature. So in the third turning there are *provisional teachings* and *definitive teachings*.[23] The provisional teachings say that all appearances are manifestations of the mind, and this was explained by Maitreya in three commentaries: *The Adornment of the Sutras, The Differentiation of Dharma and Dharmata* and *Differentiating the Middle from the Extremes*. For the ultimate meaning he gave the last of the five teachings which was the *Uttaratantra* shastra or the "Changeless Nature."[24] The *Uttaratantra* teaches that the nature of all phenomena is emptiness or *dharmadhatu*. But this emptiness is not a complete nothingness because it has clarity (Tib. *salwa*) and awareness. This clarity and awareness are the nature of Buddhahood and they are present in all beings, so all beings have the possibility of attaining Buddhahood.

In the Kagyu school there are three texts which are considered to be most important and which the third Karmapa, Rangjung Dorje, has suggested are to be studied. These are the *Uttaratantra*, the *Profound Inner Meaning*, and the *Hevajra Tantra*. The *Uttaratantra* is considered very important because it describes how Buddha nature is present in the true nature of the mind, and appearances are manifestation of the mind. Then in meditation one understands this true nature of the mind. So it is important to study this text to understand this intellectual viewpoint so that it can assist the realization from meditation.

Asanga was able to live for 150 years. Following 50 years in Tushita he studied the field of the Abhidharma and laid out the whole of the Abhidharma very clearly. Then Asanga had many fine disciples and followers, among whom was his brother Vasubhandu. So through Asanga and his followers, the meaning of the third turning of the wheel of dharma was explained and expounded very clearly for everyone to understand.

THE SIX ORNAMENTS

The monastic university of Nalanda was the focal point for the great development of the Mahayana teachings. At Nalanda from about the second to tenth centuries there were great masters. The Tengyur, which are all the shastras that were translated into Tibetan, has two sections: those that relate to the sutras and those that relate to the tantras. Practically all the works of the sutras in the Tengyur were composed at Nalanda during this particular period of time. At this time there were great masters there, of whom six or eight masters were most prominent. They are sometimes referred to as the "six ornaments" and sometimes as the "eight ornaments" of India. Nagarjuna (second century C.E.) was the most important master of these; he expounded the meaning of the second turning of the wheel of dharma; and Asanga was the main teacher for explaining the third turning of the wheel of dharma. So through this gathering of very great people at Nalanda, the Mahayana teachings were able to flourish. The six ornaments were Nagarjuna, Asanga, Gunaprabha, Aryadeva, Vasubhandu, and Sakyaprabha. If we add Dignaga and Dharmakirti, they become the eight ornaments.

In Tibet four great basic sets of Buddhist texts were studied. The first teachings concern the Madhyamaka, which established that all phenomena are empty. The second set of teachings is the Abhidharma, which gives an explanation of the way in which one has to travel through the various levels and paths that lead to enlightenment and describes what is to be realized and what is to be given up. The third main set of teachings are the Prajnaparamita teachings, which give a very detailed explanation of the levels and paths leading to enlightenment. Then the fourth section are the Vinaya teachings, which give all the rules of discipline and vows for all the different monastic ordinations.

Although the four main sets of texts are studied, one can reduce these into three sections, because the Madhyamaka and Prajnaparamita have similar subject matter and are counted together. These three mains sections of teachings can be related to the six great masters.

Three main teachers expounded each of these three basic teachings. The Madhyamaka was mainly presented and clarified by Nagarjuna. The Abhidharma was mainly presented, explained and commented on by Asanga. And the Vinaya was mainly presented and explained by Gunaprabha. Each of these three masters had a disciple who then wrote commentaries about these basic teachings and explained and commented on them further. So the work of Nagarjuna was commented on by his disciple Aryadeva. The work of Asanga was commented on by his brother Vasubhandu. And the work of Gunaprabha was commented on by Sakyaprabha. So we have three masters who expounded the root meaning of the Madhyamaka, the Abhidharma, and the Vinaya teachings, and three other masters who commented on and explained these teachings further.

There is still another aspect of the teachings, which is the aspect of logic intended to produce valid cognition or pramana in Sanskrit. The teachings on pramana are very important because this teaches one how to examine the teachings in a logical way, so that one can develop a conviction of its actual validity. The two main teachers who expounded the Pramana teachings were Dignaga and Dharmakirti.

One may wonder how these teachings relate to the practice of meditation. As already mentioned, in accordance with the sutras of the Buddha there developed the philosophy of Madhyamaka with its two aspects of empty in itself and empty of external phenomena. But what is the actual implication of this philosophy as far as our practice is concerned? What we need to know when we meditate is the actual nature of things just as they are, and we need to develop enough confidence in the fact that things are actually as they are. But for this we need to be given very clear, convincing reasons so that we can develop confidence in that kind of view. We need to develop the kind of unchanging confidence that could not even be moved by somebody else's arguments. If someone tells you, "Well, this isn't really true," you need to have such convincing reasons yourself that nobody can make you change your mind about the true view. So these teachings of Madhyamaka can help us develop that type of confidence concerning the right view for meditation.

With the Vajrayana it is slightly different. When we meditate we are no longer concerned with reasons. We just look directly at the actual nature of things. It's a matter of direct recognition much more than thinking about reasons and how things should be.

Chapter 7

THE SPREAD OF THE VAJRAYANA TEACHINGS

In the previous chapter we saw the beginning and spreading of the Mahayana teachings in India which happened mainly through the efforts of the University of Nalanda. In this chapter we will see how this was followed by a great wave of the development and spreading of the Vajrayana teachings.

THE DEVELOPMENT OF THE VAJRAYANA TEACHINGS

As previously mentioned, the Buddha turned the wheel of dharma of the Vajrayana with the four categories of tantra. We find the texts of the tantras in the Tibetan Kangyur and in the Tibetan Tengyur. Another name for the Vajrayana in Tibetan is the "secret mantra" or *sang ngak*. The syllable *ngak* is Tibetan for the Sanskrit word "mantra." The Sanskrit word "mantra" itself is composed of two syllables: *man* which means "the mind," that is, this inner mind, and *tra*, which means "that which protects" or "that which can give protection." So "mantra" can be interpreted as meaning "the means to protect the mind." The Tibetans translated this word "mantra" by the word *ngak*, which actually has the flavor of this, the idea of the possibility to change, so the Vajrayana is to achieve happiness very quickly, instantaneously without having to rely on a strong, strenuous effort with many difficulties. So it's the idea of a means that is very powerful to accomplish, a sudden change for the better.

Now the word "tantra" was translated into Tibetan as *gyu*. This word means "continuity" and refers to the continuum of the mind. The goal of practice is to gradually change this continuum from a very negative one into the very positive one of a bodhisattva or Buddha. So this state is of a continuum from our present mind. This is why it was used to translate "tantra."

What is required in the Sutrayana, the way of practicing according to the sutras, is meditation on a conviction one has gained, with a lot of diligence and effort in practice. In the Vajrayana one also needs faith and devotion, but what the Vajrayana has to offer in particular is a whole range of different techniques that make the practice very effective, so that it is possible to achieve the goal of enlightenment very quickly. In the Vajrayana one does not meditate on a mere conviction, but one is directly introduced to the nature of reality within one's own mind, using the forms of deities and many other skillful means for meditation. So the Vajrayana is very special and a great teaching because it makes it possible for us to follow a path that isn't very long and difficult. This is, however, a path intended for those who have great intelligence, faith, devotion, motivation and interest in the practice.

The teachings of the Vajrayana developed in India after the great wave of Mahayana expansion from Nalanda. Although the Vajrayana spread more or less everywhere in India, the apex of this development was the monastic University of Vikramashila, where there were the six "doorkeeper panditas." These mahapanditas were very great teachers who lived at the University of Vikramashila, and each of them lived over one of the gates of the university so they were guarding the gates in each of the directions. These mahapanditas had two main functions. One was to refute the attacks of tirthikas. Sometimes tirthikas would come to the university and they would try to refute the Vajrayana teachings either through logic or through a display of miraculous powers. So one of the tasks of these panditas guarding the gates of the university was to keep watch against these tirthikas who came to refute the teachings. Another function was to look after people who wanted to practice the dharma, and in particular, the Vajrayana teachings. So these mahapanditas had to be there to give teachings to those who were ready for that type of teaching.

Over the eastern gate of the University of Vikramashila was the mahapandita called Shantipa who sometimes was called Ratnakarashantipa. Over the southern gate was the mahapandita Prajnakaramati. Over the western gate was the mahapandita Vagishvarakirti, and then over the northern gate was the famous mahapandita Naropa. Then at the center of the monastic complex were two great pillars. In the first of these pillars lived Ratnavajra and near the second pillar lived the mahapandita Jnanashri. So these were the six mahapanditas who watched over the gates of the monastic University of Vikramashila. There were also six doorkeeper panditas at Nalanda University who held and spread the teachings in India.

The Buddhist teachings were spread in three great waves called the turning of the wheel of dharma. The first turning was done by the seven patriarchs or "holders of the transmission" who transmitted the Foundation vehicle teachings. Then when Nalanda University was at its peak, the Mahayana teachings were spread, which were the second turning. Then at the time of the University of Vikramashila, the Vajrayana teachings of the third turning were predominantly spread. However, one vehicle did not preclude the spreading of the other two vehicles. For instance, at the time of the Foundation vehicle expansion, the Mahayana or Vajrayana teachings were also practiced, but the main emphasis at the time was on the Foundation vehicle teachings. Similarly, at the time of the expansion of Mahayana teachings, the Foundation vehicle and Vajrayana were also practiced, though to a lesser degree.

We know from the biographies of the eight ornaments such as Nagarjuna and Dharmakirti that while they were propagating the Mahayana teachings at Nalanda University, they were also personally practicing the Vajrayana teachings and were able to master these Vajrayana teachings because they became great mahasiddhas.

There are three stages one goes through in Vajrayana practice, with each level having a different behavior and action associated with it. When one is a beginner in the practice, all the qualities of meditation are still not present, and one has not developed any special qualities yet, so one follows what is known as "the behavior of Samantabhadra," which is a completely wholesome behavior. During this time one's behavior should be completely positive and one should always act in a very disciplined, careful way. By the second level, one has already gained some experience and understanding of the mind through meditation, so one's energies are turned inwards, concentrated on one's practice, one's mind and one's meditation. Finally, when one has developed an extremely high degree of meditation so that one has an unusual degree of cognition and understanding and one has achieved some miraculous powers, one enters the third level called "victorious in all directions." At this time, through one's miraculous powers, one can go anywhere, do anything, emanate in any form that is required. When it is necessary to counteract the doubts or the wrong views of another, one can use miraculous powers to convince them of the rightness of the dharma. Mahasiddhas behave in a way that is completely beyond the domain of behavior of ordinary people. Some of them were seen to be riding tigers or flying in the sky and all sorts of unusual things. Whatever they did and whatever they ate, and wherever they went, was completely beyond all the rules of ordinary human behavior. One never knew quite where they were or what they were doing. Sometimes they were on a beach near the ocean and sometimes they might be in a cave. So these people entered the realm of behavior which was entirely beyond all our normal standards. They are called *siddhas,* they reached the special powers called *siddhis.*

The story of Vajraghanta illustrates these various levels of behavior of the Vajrayana. When he first started with the practice of Vajrayana, he observed all the rules of conduct very carefully. He engaged in wholesome behavior and his practice was always extremely diligent and careful. He was so remarkable in his practice that he became quite well known to the king. The king thought, "I must get this man to come to me and give me some teachings." So he sent someone to invite Vajraghanta to come to the palace to teach the king. But when Vajraghanta was told about the invitation of the king, he thought, "I have no desire whatsoever to go there because the king's palace is only like a prison to me. I don't consider this a special honor or something good. As far as the pleasures of the king's court are concerned, they are like a pit of fire to me. I don't have any desire whatsoever to go to the king's palace and prefer to stay in solitude to practice meditation."

When the news was given to the king, the king was very disappointed because he wanted so much for this man to come and teach him. So the king personally went to see Vajraghanta and asked him if he would come and teach him at the palace. But the monk Vajraghanta gave him the same answer, that he didn't want to come to the palace; that it would be just like a prison and all of the pleasures of the court would be like fire. The king was rather displeased and unhappy and left. Then Vajraghanta carried on with his practice and achieved the state of a mahasiddha. Having achieved this state, he took a wife and had a son and a daughter. He also used to drink a lot of chang, which is Tibetan beer.

Some time later the king heard that Vajraghanta was coming to town, so he assembled all the ministers, all the queens and all the people to meet him. When Vajraghanta came, the king said, "Here you are, the very virtuous, self-righteous monk. You could never bear to come to my palace to teach me because you thought it would be like a prison and all the pleasures would be like fire. Now what do I see? Who is with you?" Then Vajraghanta said, "That's my wife." Then the king and all the other people started insulting him and saying terrible things about him. Vajraghanta replied, "Don't do this because this is part of something you can't understand. This belongs to Vajrayana practice." But they wouldn't stop insulting him.

Then the king said, "Who are these children?" And Vajraghanta replied, "That's my son and that's my daughter." Again they insulted him and said all sorts of terrible things about him. Vajraghanta was carrying a pot full of chang and the king and all of the other people started insulting him because he was drinking. When Vajraghanta realized that they wouldn't stop insulting him, which is a very negative thing to do, he arose as the *mandala* of Chakrasamvara and his son and daughter turned into a vajra and a bell. The pot of beer that he was carrying turned into an immense lake of beer that covered the whole area so that everybody—the king, the queens and the ministers—started to drown in the beer. So, of course, they all started to apologize and said they regretted what they had done. As soon as they had realized their mistake, the beer stopped rising. As a result of this great miraculous display, the king and everyone were convinced of the great value of Vajrayana and received the teachings and practiced them.

Another example of the miraculous powers that come from meditation can be seen in the story of the mahasiddha Luipa who lived in a little cave just near the Ganges River. There was a large crack in his cave and one day while he was meditating, he fell into the water of the Ganges. He was still meditating when a huge fish ate him up, but he just remained there meditating inside the belly of the fish. A fisherman who was fishing on the bank of the Ganges River caught that huge fish. When the fish was killed, they found Luipa inside the fish's belly still meditating. This, of course, shows the incredible power of meditation and this mahasiddha was given the name of Luipa, which means "fish belly."

THE EIGHT MAHASIDDHAS

Eight mahasiddhas are particularly famous in India: Saraha, Nagarjuna, Kukkuripa, Vajraghanta, Birupa, Dombhi Heruka, the great King Indrabhuti, and Luipa. One finds in the *Eighty-four Mahasiddhas* that some of them are mentioned at one event and then another time 200 or 300 years later. For example, one finds the first mention of Nagarjuna in the second century C.E. and then several hundred years later Nagarjuna is mentioned again in the story of Tilopa (about 900 C.E.). The same thing with Saraha. But, in fact, there weren't two Nagarjunas or two Sarahas. It is just that these beings are completely beyond the domain of ordinary human behavior and what we can imagine. They were able to live something like 900 years. Sometimes they would live in one place for maybe 100 years and then they might go to another place and spend another 100 years there. Sometimes they might manifest in one body and sometimes they might manifest in two forms simultaneously. So it's not worth it to have doubts about these kind of things, because these mahasiddhas are completely beyond our ordinary beliefs of reality. We just can't judge them by our ordinary standards. It is because they have achieved the highest spiritual accomplishment and it is part of the power of that spiritual accomplishment that these beings are on a different level from us.

Chapter 8

THE TEN BUDDHIST SCIENCES

In this history of Buddhism in India, we saw how the Buddha was born and how by means of twelve deeds he helped beings. We saw how he turned the wheel of dharma by giving teachings in correspondence with the various aspirations and capacities of beings: the Foundation vehicle, Mahayana and Vajrayana teachings. We saw how the six ornaments and the six doorkeeper panditas lived, practiced and taught in India and how there were the eight mahasiddhas and the eighty-four mahasiddhas. Since everything that was important in the history of dharma first took place in India, India is referred to as the holy land in Tibetan works.

The teachings of the Buddha were given in the form of the three vehicles, each one with its particular view, practice and meditation. Besides these teachings of the three vehicles, there were also teachings on what is known as the ten branches of knowledge or the ten sciences. These ten branches of knowledge are not indispensable for meditation, but they can help people understand the teachings and gain a better understanding and conviction of the teachings.

These ten branches of knowledge are considered a secondary aspect of the Buddhist teachings and the ten branches of the Buddhist sciences can be divided into two categories: the five major and five minor Buddhist sciences.

The Five Major Sciences

The first of the five major Buddhist sciences is called the "inner science" or *nangdön ngpa* in Tibetan. These are all the teachings that have to do with realizing the nature of the mind. It is exactly in accordance with what the Buddha taught in the three turnings of the wheel of dharma and is intended to help us realize the true nature of the mind, to help us gain protection from suffering. So this inner science is the dharma and has already been covered in the previous chapters. The other four major and the five minor sciences are supporting limbs to the inner science, which is the main subject of the sciences.

The second major Buddhist science, called *dra* in Tibetan, is intended to get rid of all our doubts about words, about terminology. This is the science of linguistics and grammar, everything to do with words and understanding words. Whether we are dealing with the actual words of the Buddha or the words of the great teachers who wrote the shastras, we will have to understand the use of words, because it is by means of words that these teachers convey their thoughts to us. To understand what they intended to say, to grasp what they had to transmit, we have to understand the use of words and understand why they expressed themselves in such a way. So the science that makes it possible to grasp the actual meaning of the words, the power behind each word, the expressive capacity of each word, is this science of grammar and linguistics.

The third major science is logic or in Tibetan *tantsig* or *shama*, and this science helps us to get rid of doubts and uncertainties about the meaning of words. This is not just in terms of the words, but in terms of the actual meaning. In order to understand what the Buddha and the great masters were saying, one needs to see the reasons behind what they were saying, the justifications for what they were saying. One needs to understand why they said things in such a way, and what they expressed. If we can apply logic properly, then we will be able to understand more clearly what the masters had in mind, without doubts and misconceptions. That is why the third branch of Buddhist science is logic, which is also called Pramana.

The fourth major Buddhist science is the arts or *zowa* in Tibetan. The arts are a practical aspect of Buddhist science; it is necessary to make representations of the Buddha's form in either statues or drawings. One can develop more faith and devotion in the Buddha through learning these arts properly and knowing how to represent the Buddha with all his particular attributes, doing this properly according to all the rules and standards. This can also be applied in the drawing of the yidam deities. One learns how to represent the various yidams and their attributes and their mandala, and about the other deities in the mandala. Being able to represent the yidams with their attributes and their mandalas is a visual support to the creation stage (Tib. *che rim*) of meditation in which one visualizes these deities. One also learns about all the symbolism of the various attributes and forms of these yidams so one understands the qualities of mind that these deities represent. So all this is contained in the fourth major science, the arts.

The fifth major Buddhist science is medicine or *sowa* in Tibetan. Here one examines how the nature of the body is pervaded by the suffering of illness, how transient illnesses can be caused by the three poisons, and so on. Since everything in the universe is naturally interdependent, there are methods to try to cure the illness affecting us by using substances or medicines found in the outer world. So diagnosis and treatment of illness is the task of medicine.

In India at the time of the Buddha there were already various aspects of these last four branches of knowledge, but they were not particularly Buddhist, having been developed by non-Buddhists. So the particular Buddhist aspect of these sciences was gradually developed by various Buddhist teachers. The second major science, linguistics, developed with the study of the Sanskrit language, because that language was used at the time for the teachings.[25] The main work started at Nalanda with a great teacher called acarya Chandragomin. He was a teacher and also a bodhisattva, but didn't take the full ordination of a monk. He had taken all the vows of a lay disciple and that is why he was called "Gomin," which is a word that designates a particular kind of lay disciple. He composed the first important shastra on linguistics, which was called *Candra Nyakarana*.

Another teacher, Saptavarman, composed another shastra on linguistics called the *Kalapa Vyakarana*. Also in the south of India there was a teacher called acarya Anubhuti, and he had a direct, pure vision of the female deity Sarasvati. She transmitted to him directly a very important text that was to be the whole basis of grammar and linguistics in Sanskrit and that was later on extremely useful at the time when all the teachings were translated into Tibetan. This shastra was called the *Sarasrata*

Vyakarana. These three main shastras provided the whole basis for linguistics and grammar.

The third major science, that of logic, is intended to help us develop great trust, confidence and conviction in the Buddha's teaching. There are two aspects of this science of logic: "direct cognition," which occurs when the mind can grasp whatever is looked at directly, and "inferential cognition," which occurs when things are understood correctly through inference. Through these two aspects one can develop the conviction that the Buddha's teachings and the shastras are correct. When the Buddha taught and later when the shastras were composed, there wasn't the science of pramana, this science of valid cognition. Logical analyses were referred to, but didn't deal with it at any length. So later on, in order to clarify this topic and explain it in more detail, one of the eight ornaments of India, Dignaga, wrote a work called the *Pramanasamuccaya*, which deals with this valid cognition. Then after Dignaga, Dharmakirti wrote seven shastras on the intention of Dignaga, making logic very widely known.

When Dignaga was writing the *Pramanasamuccaya* he first started writing out the notes and began saying, "To him who has become valid reason itself, who knows what is of benefit to beings, to the teacher Buddha I prostrate." Thus he was praising the Buddha for two reasons, one that he understood everything in a perfectly valid way, and second that he had great compassion for sentient beings. These two qualities make the Buddha a worthy object of prostration. But when he came back the next day to carry on with his work, he found that these words had disappeared. This was because there was a tirthika teacher who through his negative miraculous powers had erased them. So he wrote them out again. But next time he came, he found them gone again, because the tirthika teacher had erased them again. Then Dignaga wondered whether whoever was doing this was just playing a game or if he was really trying to challenge him in some way. So he wrote down, "Whoever you are, if you are just playing, then stop fooling around because what I'm doing is important. But if you're trying to challenge me, then please come and let's have a debate. A debate will be more positive." Then the tirthika teacher called Krisnamuniraja came saying he'd like to have a debate. So the debate between Krisnamuniraja and Dignaga took place and Dignaga defeated his opponent. It was after this that he finished writing his work the *Pramanasamuccaya*, and after this the science of Pramana was able to develop and spread.

The fourth major branch of knowledge is the arts. The very first image of the Buddha was made during his lifetime. The daughter of the king of Sri Lanka (or Ceylon) had heard of the Buddha. Although she had never met the Buddha, just hearing his name made her feel tremendous faith in the Buddha, and so she wrote to him. The Buddha, seeing that it was time to lead some of the people in Sri Lanka onto the path of dharma, did a special miracle on a piece of cloth that the daughter of the king had. With the light from the Buddha's body there appeared on the cloth the whole form of the Buddha's body and a verse of the Buddha's words. As soon as the king's daughter saw this, she immediately realized the true nature of phenomena. Following this, the teachings of the Buddha were able to spread in Sri Lanka. So this first form of the Buddha appeared on the cloth and was afterwards used as the standard for representing the Buddha's features. There are many different stories about the development of the art of representing the Buddha's form, but they won't be given here.[26]

The fifth major science is medicine. There was mention of some elements of medicine in the Buddha's first turning of the wheel of dharma when he was teaching the Vinaya. In the Vinaya there are some expositions of various types of medicines and remedies that heal the body and bring about a better state of health and well-being. Later, at the time when the University of Nalanda was flourishing, there was a *rishi* living in the forest near Nalanda who was actually an emanation of the medicine Buddha. He taught the four great tantras on medical science: the root tantra, the explanatory tantra, the instruction tantra and the later tantra. They represent the basis from which medical science later developed in Tibet.

The Five Minor Sciences

The main minor science is astrology, known in Tibet as *tsi*. Astrology has a general aspect which studies the movement of the planets and the stars, and according to these movements one can determine what will be the fate or the events that will take place in the world in a given period of time. This also has an individual application, insofar as when one knows the time of birth of a given person, one can predict the various happenings in that person's life: what is likely to be good, what is likely to be difficult. The value of this is that if one faces a lot of difficulty, one can try to find out how one can avert the difficulties that might otherwise arise. Then there is also an application in predicting what may happen every year. Each year there is a different disposition of the external elements and the inner elements of a person. According to the correspondence between these outer and inner elements there are different possibilities for either sickness or absence of sickness each year. So once you know what is likely to happen within a given year, then you can try to apply the means that will change the course of events if they are going to be very bad. Astrology can also be used to see whether the elements are in harmony for two people who plan to get married.

The actual source of this science of astrology is to be found in the Kalachakra Tantra. The Kalachakra Tantra has three aspects, an outer aspect, an inner aspect, and a secret aspect. The outer aspect describes the movements of the various planets and stars. The inner aspect of the tantra explains the essential nature of phenomena. And the secret aspect describes the mandala of the deities. So from the Kalachakra Tantra the science of astrology developed and then spread in Tibet.

A second minor Buddhist science is poetry or *nyan ngak* in Tibetan. Of course when one writes any work or any teaching, one needs to know how to write according to the proper style. But when it comes to writing a prayer or a spiritual song, or any text that is intended to really stir something deeply inside or to kindle devotion and conviction, then it is very necessary to know how to use poetry. This is why poetry is one of the minor arts of Buddhism. Poetry wasn't actually used directly in any of the sutras, but it is found indirectly in various Buddhist works.

The actual development of Buddhist poetry goes back to the time of Nalanda. In the previously given story about Aryadeva, who was challenged by Matriceta and his parrot, Matriceta was eventually defeated in the debate. The tradition of those days was that the one who was defeated had to embrace the faith of the victor. But it was very difficult for Matriceta to be really convinced to become a Buddhist. He couldn't really become a Buddhist from the heart. According to the tradition, he was kept at Nalanda until he embraced the faith properly. They decided to lock him up in the library at Nalanda. Of course, days are very long when you are on your own in a library like this. Matriceta got so bored that he started taking all the books off the shelves and leafing through them, looking here and looking there. In the end, with all the things he read, he developed tremendous faith in the Buddha because he thought, "Well, the Buddha was really an amazing being and what he says is really outstanding." He was so impressed that he composed a book called the *Jatakamala* containing the thirty-four stories of the previous lives of the Buddha[27] and this is actually the first real work of poetry in the Buddhist tradition. The first story in it is about when the Buddha gave his body to a tigress when he was a prince in a previous life.[28]

The third minor Buddhist science is of meter or *deb djor* in Tibetan, and this science tells one just how long the verses should be, what length or weight they should have in a sentence and so on. So it tells you just how you should balance the words out and what kind of meter should be used.

The fourth minor science is that of the tradition of making up a thesaurus or *ngön djöd* in Tibetan. It's a book that contains all the various synonyms needed. If you have one word, then it gives you another five or six other words that mean the same thing.

And the fifth minor science is that of sacred dances or *dö gar* in Tibetan. Strangely, the tradition of religious dancing didn't spread to Tibet at the time when Buddhism was introduced, because the Tibetan scholars did not consider dancing to be very important and did not care to translate it. So it didn't go to Tibet at the time.

These last three minor sciences of meter, thesaurus making, and sacred dances aren't set out in separate works or particular shastras, but are found here and there in different works.

Chapter 9

BODHGAYA AND THE BUDDHA ESSENCE

What is the purpose of a Buddhist pilgrimage?[29] To begin with, the Buddha appeared in India and achieved complete and perfect Buddhahood there. Having achieved complete and perfect enlightenment, he then turned the wheel of the dharma. Buddhists, in remembrance of his activity, therefore make pilgrimages to places that the Buddha had visited. The purpose of our doing so is so that we will remember the Buddha's good qualities.

We begin by visiting the place where Buddha achieved enlightenment, to see how he achieved enlightenment, and then we go on to visit the various places where he turned the wheel of the dharma. In this way, we develop some awareness and mindfulness of the exalted activity of the Buddha. The purpose of our doing so is that through remembering and being mindful of the Buddha's deeds, we ourselves are encouraged so that our strength of heart will increase, our longing and admiration for the dharma will increase. Because of this we will enter into the practice of the dharma with great effort, and through practicing, we may achieve the final fruition of the dharma. We call this receiving the blessing of the Buddha or the blessing of these sacred places, or from a worldly point of view, we can say by just recollecting the history of the Buddhist tradition we will develop the aspiration to practice and achieve the fruition. There are, in any case, a great many reasons for going on pilgrimage.

Generally speaking, in this world, which we refer to as Jambudvipa in the Buddhist tradition, there are many different religious traditions. There is a purpose and need for all of these various religious traditions. Non-Buddhist traditions usually believe in a god or a deity. In theistic traditions, when we please that deity we achieve happiness; and by displeasing that deity we incur suffering. However, in the Buddhist way we think about it differently. In the Buddhist tradition we believe the experience of pain and pleasure or happiness and suffering comes about as the fruition of an individual's actions or karma. In the Buddhist tradition we speak about abandoning negative or wicked states of mind (called kleshas) and, by abandoning these kleshas, we achieve the final fruition of awakening or enlightenment. The Buddha then is a teacher of how to do this and he is the one who gave these teachings.

The Buddha did not begin as a deity. He began as an ordinary, common being. He generated within himself the aspiration to complete enlightenment for the sake of all sentient beings, called "the mind of enlightenment" or bodhichitta in Sanskrit. Having generated bodhichitta, he began to accumulate the two collections, the accumulation of wisdom and the accumulation of merit. Having completed the collections, he achieved the final fruition. Following his example, many other accomplished persons, great bodhisattvas, achieved the final fruition. Similarly, people such as ourselves, even though we are not great bodhisattvas (we are just ordinary people), nevertheless, by following the various methods that the Buddha taught, we too can generate this aspiration for enlightenment for the sake of all sentient beings; having done so we too can accumulate the collections of wisdom and merit and, through accumulating wisdom and merit, bring into manifestation the complete and perfect enlightenment that was achieved by the Buddha.

When we say "Buddha," we are speaking about the fruition. In Tibetan the word that we use for Buddha is *Sang-gyä* and those two syllables refer to the two aspects of the good qualities of the Buddha. Whether we are thinking about this in terms of Buddha Shakyamuni, the one who has already achieved Buddhahood, or whether we are thinking about the Buddhahood that we ourselves will achieve in the future, it is the same. It is indeed suitable, appropriate and possible for people such as ourselves to achieve Buddhahood.

At this point we have, however, the obstruction of the various disturbing emotions (Skt. *kleshas*) that exist within our mind. The principal obstruction is called ignorance. Because of ignorance the various other disturbing emotions arise in the mind, such as desire, hatred, pride, and envy. Ignorance gives rise to two sorts of obstructions, (a) the afflictive obstructions, or klesha-vadana in Sanskrit, and (b) the obstructions with regard to knowledge, or vijnana-vadana. It is because of those two obstructions—the emotional obstructions and the obstructions to knowledge—that we are not able to achieve enlightenment and that we remain in samsara, where we have to undergo all sorts of suffering from all sorts of difficult situations and conditions. In that way, there is a relationship of cause and effect. The cause, ignorance, gives rise to the effect, suffering within samsara. Therefore we need to eliminate those obstructions. That is what the first syllable *sang* in the Tibetan means. *Sang* means something like "cleanse" and refers to clearing away, removing, or abandoning these various sorts of obstructions. When that has been done, then various good qualities manifest. If we are speaking about ourselves and say *sang*, then we are talking about the need to separate ourselves from these obstructions. If we are speaking about the Buddha and we say *sang*, then we are referring to the fact that he has already done so.

By purifying the obstructions in this way, all the good qualities are brought into a manifest state; the good qualities and wisdom (Skt. *jnana*) are generated or born within us. When all of the good qualities without exception have been generated within us, then that is Buddhahood, which is what the second syllable in the word *Sang-gyä* refers to. *Gyä* means "expand, spread, or develop extensively." When we say that the Buddha is *Sang-gyä*, we are referring to the fact that all these good qualities have been developed in a complete and manifest form.

Just as the Buddha accomplished enlightenment, so we too are able to practice the path and accomplish enlightenment. The reason is that whatever causes enabled Buddha to achieve enlightenment, whatever causes existed within the Buddha's stream of being, exist identically in us. This is summarized when the Buddha said: "All sentient beings have the Buddha essence."

However, it is not apparent that this Buddha essence exists within all sentient beings. Because if we look at ourselves, we see that we have this fairly crude, ordinary body, this unrefined speech and this fairly confused ordinary mind. Looking through our body, speech, and mind, we don't see anything we would call the "essence of the Buddha." What we see, rather, is something impermanent, impure, and dirty. So, we may wonder, "Where is this Buddha essence? It doesn't exist. I can't find it. I can't see it." However, if you settle this, fundamentally, take this right down to the very basis, then you can understand that the Buddha essence does indeed exist in all sentient beings.

These experiences that we have of body, speech, and mind are appearances based on a fundamental ignorance that we have. Because ignorance covers and conceals the true nature, we are not able to see the true nature of body, speech, and mind. Rather, we have mistaken and confused experiences. To respond to that the Buddha in the *Heart Sutra* said, "There is no eye, no ear, no nose, no tongue, no body, no mind, no form, no feeling" and so forth. He was saying all of these lack inherent existence; they are not established by way of their own nature. They are empty of any nature of their own. As truths for a concealing consciousness, all of these things appear, together with both actions or karma and their effect. So speaking about this in the context of what are known as the two truths, we say that various sorts of appearances do dawn (relative truth): eye, ear, nose, tongue, body, mind, visible forms, sounds, smells, tastes, tangible objects and so forth. All these things do appear, dawn and arise, however, ultimately their mode of abiding is that they are like dreams, they are not established and they do not exist (ultimate truth).

All these various kinds of appearances are not established by way of their own nature, they are empty of any such nature. Their emptiness, their lack of any inherent existence, was demonstrated with reasoning by many great scholars and learned persons in the past, such as Nagarjuna, Asanga, and Chandrakirti. However, if we just speak about this from the viewpoint of the experience that we ourselves have, it is like a dream. In a dream all sorts of things appear: visual forms, feelings, sounds, smells, tastes, tangible objects. All of these things do indeed appear very vividly. But they are just dream appearances, being false and not true. They are not what they *seem* to be. For example, when we are dreaming we can imagine that we are in a very nice house where everything is very pleasant, well arranged, and delightful. But in fact we are sleeping and we are just in our own ordinary house. The objects and feelings in our dream seem to be appearing very vividly; they appear to be real. In waking life both our body and the external world *appear* as if they were really and truly existent and established. But in fact, they do not exist, nevertheless, they do appear. They appear, they arise, but they are not established, they do not exist. Ultimately then all phenomena are emptiness, all of these impure phenomena that we experience are emptiness.

What is the nature of this emptiness? Is it an utter non-existence that is a mere voidness? No, that is not what it is. Space, for instance, is voidness, but space is not something that allows various phenomena to appear, to arise, and to dawn. It doesn't have any factor of luminous clarity (Tib. *salwa*). Space is just a dead emptiness. This non-existence of phenomena that we call emptiness is also what we call by the name *chö-ji-yin* or dharmadhatu, where *yin* or dhatu has the meaning of "space, realm, sphere within which all good qualities can arise, within which anything could arise, could appear, could dawn." Impure phenomena could arise, pure phenomena could arise. It is entirely suitable, possible or appropriate for any sort of phenomena to appear within that dharmadhatu or "sphere of reality." That luminous clarity then is the basis for wisdom or jnana.

We speak then about the union of space and wisdom or the union of this *yin* or dhatu and wisdom. It is an inseparability of luminous clarity and emptiness. Because the nature of this union of wisdom and space is emptiness, stains and defilements are suitable to be abandoned. And because luminous clarity is the nature of this dharmadhatu or sphere of reality, all good qualities are suitable to arise or to be generated in it. This union of space and wisdom, of luminous clarity and emptiness, pervades all sentient beings. It is in the light of this that we say that Buddha essence pervades all sentient beings or that all sentient beings have this Buddha essence.

This inseparable union of space and wisdom is also called by the name "sugatagarbha," which means "the essence of the one gone to bliss" with *garbha* meaning "essence" and *sugata* the name for the Buddha, the one gone to bliss. We say it pervades all sentient beings because the sugatagarbha exists in all sentient beings, and the adventitious defilements (those defilements which are not part of the true nature of mind), can be cleared away. Thus, in the *Uttaratantra* or the text on "The Hierarchy of Being that Exists within all Sentient Beings," it is said, "All sentient beings are Buddha, however, these adventitious defilements obstruct Buddhahood."

Sugatagarbha is discussed in the *Uttaratantra* in terms of four different topics: (1) The nature of the sugatagarbha, which is as I have just explained. Through listening to such presentations, contemplating their meaning and then meditating upon what one has understood, it is possible to achieve the fruition or effect. (2) Having realized the sugatagarbha and having cultivated the path of that realization, one gradually achieves the bodhi or *changchub*, "enlightenment," which is the second of the four topics in terms of which the sugatagarbha is explained. (3) When one achieves enlightenment, then various good qualities come along, because the enlightenment that one achieves is of the very nature of emptiness and luminous clarity which has been brought into a manifest state. (4) Finally, the Buddha's enlightened activity is described in terms of the three bodies of the Buddha.

When we speak about the nature of this enlightenment, we begin first in terms of the extraordinary good qualities that a Buddha possesses. We could elaborate and name these qualities for quite a long time. But we can summarize the extraordinary and marvelous qualities of a Buddha's mind as knowledge, tender love, and capacity or power.

The first quality, a Buddha's knowledge, is related to the luminous clarity that is the very nature of the Buddha's mind and of enlightenment. This exalted knowledge of a Buddha is able to recognize, know, to cognize all phenomena whatsoever, both conventional phenomena and ultimate phenomena. There is nothing whatsoever that is obscured from a Buddha; there are no objects of knowledge that a Buddha does not know; there is no obstruction of anything by anything whatsoever because a Buddha knows conventional and ultimate phenomena. With this knowledge a Buddha sees the situation that various sentient beings find themselves having to endure and the sort of suffering that they have to undergo simply because of being mistaken about the basic nature of reality. By seeing the suffering of sentient beings a Buddha's tender love comes forth. We say that if the Buddhas just had knowledge and love for sentient beings but had no capacity to do anything for them then it would not be of much use. But because of knowledge and love, the Buddhas are able to have tremendous capacity, tremendous power. Through that sort of capacity or power, a Buddha is able to help sentient beings.

That was a brief presentation of the good qualities of a Buddha's mind. We could also speak about the good qualities of a Buddha's body and speech. If we speak about a Buddha's body, then the good qualities are described in terms of the thirty-two primary and the eighty supplementary qualities.

The fourth topic is called "the Buddha's enlightened activity" and is described in terms of the three bodies or kayas of the Buddha. These are: (a) The dharmakaya, *chö-ku* in Tibetan, or "truth body."(b) The body that appears to students who are said to be pure, those who have achieved a high level. That body is called the sambhogakaya, the "complete enjoyment body." (c) The nirmanakaya or "emanation body" appears from the perspective of students who are in an impure state: in particular, from among the many types of nirmanakaya there is the enlightened activity carried out by the supreme nirmanakaya, which demonstrates the deeds of achieving enlightenment, turning the wheel of dharma and so forth.

Questions

Question: I have a question about the relationship between pilgrimage and purification practice?
Rinpoche: The purification of ill deeds and obstructions and an increase of good qualities depend mainly upon oneself. Why is that? When we go to places where the Buddha himself went, the place where he was born, the place where he passed away and so forth, if one has faith and longing with devotion toward Buddha, then if one goes to those places and thinks about it, then one will find that one's confidence in the dharma, one's certainty about the dharma, and exertion for practicing the dharma will increase. If these arise in that way, trust, certainty and exertion, then similarly one's samadhi and one's prajna will also increase. If one does not have such faith, respect and devotion, then there won't be any benefit. For instance, think about all the beggars in Bodhgaya. They don't have that kind of faith, respect and longing for the

dharma, so even though they stay in this most holy place all the time, except for generating more hatred and more kleshas, there is no benefit whatsoever for them. They don't develop any faith in the Buddha. So, when you look at that you see what it depends upon. All the beggars think about is how many rupees they can get each day. Then they start quarrelling with each other; there is a lot of agitation and there is no benefit because they have no faith in the Buddha. So you can see that it comes down to one's own motivation.

We can see that for all Buddhists throughout the history of the Buddhadharma who have come on pilgrimage, and for practitioners of the tradition, wherever they might be, there is a great deal of benefit from going on pilgrimage. How is that? Consider the example of the Chinese monk called Huien Tsiang, the one who wrote an account of his visit to all these sacred places of the Buddhist tradition in India. He went to all these sacred places and wrote an extensive account of his visit. And that has been of tremendous benefit to all Buddhists in all traditions. So, there is a great deal of benefit from going on pilgrimage.

Now we have gone to important places and have undergone hardships to do this. I am very glad about this. You have shown real faith and longing for the dharma. You have put forth exertion in this pilgrimage. I am extremely pleased, glad, delighted and happy. It is really very delightful and extremely good fortune. Particularly, if you come from a Western country where there is real prosperity, good roads, and comfortable travel, it is very difficult to come to India, which hasn't prospered in the way the countries in the West have prospered. The Indian roads are awful and everything is filthy. But these are the only roads there are and if you don't go on these roads, you are not going to go. The only thing one can do is to realize that these are the roads there are;

there are no other roads to get to these places. So then you have an attitude of patience and forbearance, going along with the difficulties with endurance and bear the hardships in that way. If you don't, then there is no benefit and you will only think and talk about the fact that the roads are awful.

There are differences between traveling in the West and traveling in India. In the West, when you are traveling along the road, you stop at a service station, you go to a nice clean bathroom, you wash your hands and face nicely afterwards. Here, they don't have anything like that and you don't have any choice because it is a poor country which hasn't developed and prospered as countries in the West have. However, our purpose in doing this is with regard to the dharma. So, the main thing to think about is the dharma, to turn one's mind toward the dharma. We therefore take on this hardship voluntarily. Whether the country is poor or rich doesn't matter; this is the country in which the Buddha appeared and taught and therefore there is a great blessing. When we travel on pilgrimage, we supplicate, make aspiration prayers and undertake this joyfully; then there is a real benefit. If we just complain about the road, then there is no purpose.

Despite the fact of being in a country where the environment is difficult, we are going about it in the best way possible. If we just look and see how most people travel, the sort of buses and trains they go on and the restaurants where they eat, they are filthy. I didn't see any point in our doing it that way. We have taken a good bus, we went on the best roads we could find, we ate at clean restaurants, and truly, for a poor country where conditions aren't splendid our situation is good. We are very fortunate, so I would request you to please have an attitude of contentment.

Chapter 10

SARNATH AND THE FOUR NOBLE TRUTHS

Varanasi is the place where the Buddha first turned the wheel of dharma and taught the four noble truths, so I will talk about the Four Noble Truths.

How should one listen to a presentation of the excellent and sacred dharma? One's motivation is extremely important and on this particular occasion, the motivation, called bodhichitta, "the mind of enlightenment," the aspiration to accomplish complete enlightenment for the sake of all sentient beings throughout all of space, is of great importance. If one's motivation is not pure, then when one listens to a presentation of the dharma, whatever understanding one brings away is like a reflection of the real thing, not the real thing. Moreover, even if one has a pure motivation, but is interested only in one's own welfare, then that is a very narrow way to approach things, which we call the Hinayana motivation. It would not be appropriate for us who have had the extraordinary fortune of entering the gateway of the dharma of the Mahayana to listen to the dharma with such an attitude. Rather, we should listen to the presentation of the dharma bearing in mind the welfare of all sentient beings throughout all of space, wishing to accomplish perfect and complete enlightenment for their sake so that we can help all other sentient beings attain the state of liberation. We should have this attitude at this time. So, thinking about all beings and arousing bodhichitta one is then ready to receive this presentation of the excellent dharma.

Many different religious traditions have spread in this world. Most of which are concerned with achieving happiness and avoiding pain through pleasing a deity who is regarded as the creator of the world. The view of these religious traditions is that if one pleases that deity, then one will receive happiness, comfort, pleasure, and generally a very delightful situation. If one does not do so, by displeasing that deity, one will have suffering and a very difficult situation. So, to please that deity, practitioners of these various religious traditions engage in offerings, supplications, and so forth.

The tradition taught by our teacher, the completely enlightened Buddha, is different from that. The Buddha taught that there is no deity who is the creator of this world; rather, all these appearances arise in dependence upon ignorance and confusion, upon being mistaken about the true nature of things. Therefore, what one needs to do to achieve a state of happiness is to abandon that ignorance and confusion. Having done so, one will achieve the final happiness. In order to abandon a mistaken view, which has produced all sorts of appearances in this world, one needs to realize the true nature of abiding of phenomena, one needs to realize the nature that is actually the "truth" of phenomena. By doing so, one will be able to abandon that which needs to be abandoned. The Buddha taught the true nature of things or, phenomena, with the four truths. Later on the Buddha also spoke about the two truths. Both of these sets of truths are teaching the true nature, the way in which things actually exist. The teaching on the four truths, which are almost universally called the Four Noble Truths was given first, and so it will be discussed here.

THE FOUR NOBLE TRUTHS

The four truths are (1) suffering, (2) its origin, (3) cessation, and (4) the path leading to cessation.

1. The Truth of Suffering

The Four Thoughts that Turn the Mind Away from Samsara

The first noble truth is suffering, and this suffering has four characteristics: impermanence, suffering, emptiness and selflessness. The origin of suffering is a cause of worldly appearances, of samsara. If we are speaking about the dharma that spread to Tibet, we need to consider the way the dharma was practiced in the context of the Vajrayana. Now, suffering is to be known as suffering, the origin of suffering is to be abandoned, the cessation of suffering actualized and the path that leads to cessation practiced. The way these were practiced in the tradition of the Vajrayana as this spread in Tibet was by way of what are known as "the four thoughts that turn the mind away from samsara." These four are: (a) the difficulty of finding a situation that is free and well-favored, (b) death and impermanence, (c) karma and its effect, action and its effect, and (d) the disadvantages of samsara or cyclic existence.

The main point of the four reminders or thoughts that turn the mind away from cyclic existence or samsara is impermanence. The Buddha said that suffering is truly the nature of samsara and that we need to understand this. We need to understand that suffering is the characteristic or definitive mark of samsara. So, learned persons and practitioners of the past have focused upon the teachings of impermanence as a way to impress upon their minds what the basic nature of samsara is, recognizing that which is impermanent as impermanent. If we do not recognize that which is impermanent as impermanent, then we will become attached to the various appearances of samsara which may lead to temporary happiness that seems to be happiness but really isn't. If we become attached to these appearances of samsara, we will fall under their power. Having fallen under their power, we will not be able to enter into the dharma. And not being able to enter the dharma, we will not practice. For that reason, it is very important to know the impermanent as impermanent.

Some who hear this message about impermanence and its characteristic of emptiness and selflessness may think, "The goal of dharma ought to be that a person's courage increases and that their strength of heart increases. However, the effect of this teaching on impermanence is that a person becomes cowardly and less confident. They believe that saying the world is impermanent means that they are without a self, that they are empty. Instead of their mind becoming more courageous, they become more cowardly and they become discouraged." This is the way many people think. However, there is a good reason and purpose to stress impermanence right at the beginning.

The purpose for the Buddha to teach impermanence and selflessness is that these are the actual characteristics of things. If permanence and happiness were the actual definitive characteristics of samsara, then there would be no purpose in the Buddha saying that impermanence and suffering were the nature of such things. It is not the case, however, that permanence and pleasure are the nature of things; rather impermanence and suffering are their actual characteristic. Even though they are truly the characteristics of samsara, we tend not to recognize this as its actual character. And in teaching impermanence and suffering as the nature of things, the Buddha is introducing us to the truth about them. He has said, "It is a way of making it possible for one to achieve a great kingdom through recognizing the actual nature of the things of samsara."

Let me give an example. Suppose there was a poisonous snake right next to where I am sitting and I didn't know about it. As long as I didn't know about it, I would be sitting there comfortably and happily while there is a great danger that I am not aware of. Gradually this poisonous snake comes closer and closer and then bites me. After it did I would find myself in a very difficult situation with a lot of pain and hardship and without any method for healing the injury that had been done to me. If, on the other hand, someone were to say to me, "There is a poisonous snake right near you," even though it might be alarming and painful to hear, nevertheless, it would allow me to escape from the danger and not to have to undergo that kind of hardship. Using this example, you can see why it is that the Buddha and the spiritual friends of the past taught initially that impermanence and suffering are the nature of the things of samsara. It was so that it is possible to turn away from and flee from these dangers. So, there is a real purpose in our understanding or knowing these things to be the truth.

Impermanence is the definitive mark of samsara and, if we consider the lifetime of human beings in particular, we see that the lifetime of human beings is short. For instance, there are some turtles that live to be 300 or 400 years old. Are there any human beings that live to be 300 or 400 years old? Well, not except those who do so through some very unusual magical feats! So, from that point of view, the lifetime of human beings is very short. In that short lifetime, it is extremely important to practice the dharma so we can pass beyond the impermanence and suffering of samsara. Is it possible for us to cross over this ocean of cyclic existence, to cross to the far shore and achieve freedom from this impermanent, painful, and unsatisfying condition? Well, if we were talking about those who have been born as an animal or as a hungry ghost, it is not possible for them to do that. However, our situation of a human birth is not like theirs. We have the very good fortune and situation of having achieved the body of a human being, with which we are able to practice the dharma of the Buddha. We have the intelligence or prajna with which it is possible for us to understand those things that are to be taken up and those things that are to be discarded. And it is from this point of view that the teachers and spiritual friends of the past have said such a human lifetime is a case of having found a situation that is both free and well favored, that it is extremely difficult to find and attain and yet one has done so. Having done that it is extremely important and meaningful; it is an extremely fortunate situation. It is the basis for liberation from the difficult situation of samsara; it is the basis which one can use to go from cyclic existence to a state of freedom.

So, we have the human body that is the method or the upaya for achieving liberation from cyclic existence, which has the nature of impermanence and pain. How then shall we practice? Shall we focus upon achieving the happiness that is included within samsara and abandoning the unpleasant and manifestly painful situations of samsara? Is that the way to go about it? No, the happiness of samsara is not very stable, and the sort of happiness and pleasure we need is something beyond that, that has crossed over the ocean of such temporary happiness, that is something other than ephemeral happiness that occurs within samsara. The learned and accomplished persons of the past have talked about the disadvantageous, unsatisfying, and faulty nature of samsara, saying, "Well, in samsara there are both suffering and pleasure. As for the suffering, it is suffering. But as for the pleasure of samsara, it is just that and nothing more. There is no more promise beyond that. Whatever amount of happiness one achieves is not very stable in its nature so achieving this temporary happiness is not of any great benefit and meaning. What one needs to do is to cross beyond samsara and achieve the happiness of what is known as 'nirvana.'" Nirvana literally means "to pass beyond suffering." Nirvana is to achieve some other kind of happiness that has benefit. This is briefly the way the faults and disadvantageous aspects of samsara are explained.

Is it possible to abandon the suffering of samsara? Is it possible to cross over, to pass beyond the suffering of samsara? Yes, it is possible to abandon that suffering. If the world had been created by a god or deity, then we would be helpless because it would not be within our own power to do much about our own situation. It would not be within our own sphere of activity to either abandon suffering or to achieve real happiness. However, it is not the case that there is some deity who has created the world and put us in this situation, so we can do something about it. That is because our present condition is the fruit of our own actions; those actions are the cause that has created our suffering and therefore it is within our power to abandon the causes of suffering and to achieve the causes of happiness. If, for instance, we hear about the great suffering of beings in the lower realms and are frightened by that, is it within our own power to prevent us having that kind of suffering? Yes, it is within our power because ill deeds and non-virtuous actions are the cause of taking birth in a lower realm. And it is within our own power not to engage in such ill deeds and unfavorable activities.

If, on the other hand, we wish to enjoy the happiness of the higher realms of samsara, is it possible to do that? Yes, because the practice of virtuous actions is the cause of taking birth in a comfortable and pleasant higher realm. In that way, it is within our own power to do what we want to do and possible to achieve what we want to achieve. Suppose we want to achieve nirvana or the state of having crossed beyond all suffering of samsara altogether, is that something that we can do? Yes, by simply engaging in the causes that lead to nirvana we can do so. This then is the discussion of karma, the relationship between cause and effect.

The Buddha turned the wheel of dharma initially and explained the Four Noble Truths and particular the truth of suffering. As I said before, in Tibet where the tradition of the Vajrayana was most widely practiced, this teaching on suffering was taught mainly in terms of the practice of the four thoughts that reverse one's mind from samsara. First we begin by trying to understand these four reminders. Having understood them, we then meditate upon them. We do not meditate on them just a few times because we have to make these reminders extremely clear and vivid in our mind by meditating again and again until we have become extremely familiar with them. We do this to the point that these reminders actually rest and abide in our mind giving us great confidence in understanding their meaning. So that is the way in which this truth of suffering is to be approached.

2. The Origin of Suffering

The second among the four truths is the origin of suffering. This can be understood in terms of karma (action) and kleshas (disturbing emotions).

The various kinds of pleasure and pain that we experience in samsara lead back to our actions, karma. Since we already accumulate various kinds of negative or bad karma, we need to stop doing that and instead begin to achieve wholesome, good karma. There is a method for achieving favorable rather than unfavorable karma and this is through developing an antidote to the kleshas and thereby abandoning the kleshas.

It is with this in mind that the Buddha said that the origin of suffering is to be abandoned. The purpose in abandoning the kleshas is because they are the origin of suffering. The reason is that the kleshas such as passion, aggression, and pride never produce anything beneficial; they just produce hardships for oneself and others. They don't put one in a state of happiness and comfort. Is there a way to abandon these kleshas? One could simply say, "I am not going to be desirous," or "I am not going to become angry?" but that will not do. Rather, one has to get at the very root of desire, hatred, and so forth. There are various types of methods that are taught for abandoning the root of kleshas. There are some that are taught in the context of the paths of the Shravaka vehicle, some that are taught in the context of the great vehicle or Mahayana vehicle and others that are taught in the context of the Vajrayana vehicle. Then there are various methods that are not, properly speaking, the paths of any of those three vehicles, rather, they are just methods for temporarily suppressing, literally "pressing down the head," by temporarily taming the kleshas without actually getting rid of them from the root.

What methods are taught in the Hinayana or Shravaka vehicle for abandoning the root of the kleshas? In the tradition of the Shravaka vehicle, we first recognize the kleshas and that they are the root and cause of samsara. The Buddha taught that to abandon the kleshas we must abandon the conception of a self of a person, which is the root of the afflictions.

From beginningless time in samsara we have regarded that which does not have a self as having a self. What we need to do is to understand that there is no self, that the person is not established as a self and does not exist as a self. We have not realized this since beginningless time in samsara, so we find ourselves in a situation in which that conception of a self or person gives rise to many different kinds of kleshas. If we realize the self as actually being empty, then the various sorts of kleshas, such as desire, pride, envy and so forth, will be abandoned. When the root of the afflictions is cut, then the afflictions will not be generated. This is a brief outline of the way in which the kleshas are abandoned within the paths of the tradition of the Hinayana or Shravaka.

In the Mahayana it is said that the conception of things or phenomena is the root of kleshas. Not having recognized the true nature of things by taking external objects to be real, not realizing that they are empty, and not understanding that fact, causes one to conceive of them to be real and believe that external objects are actual things. This is confused and mistaken. We have to understand that all of the things of samsara are devoid of any nature of their own; they lack inherent existence, they are primordially unborn. In the *Prajnaparamita* sutras that set forth transcendent wisdom, the principal concept that is taught is emptiness (Skt. *shunyata*). In that way, it is explained, as it says in the *Heart Sutra*, "There is no eye, no ear, no nose, no tongue, no body, no mind, no form, no feeling" and so forth. If one meditates upon that emptiness and realizes it, one will be able to abandon the kleshas. That is the sort of path that is taught for abandoning the kleshas in the tradition of the Mahayana.

In the Mahayana, one listens to the presentation of the nature of phenomena and one contemplates the meaning of that until one accepts that emptiness is indeed the nature of phenomena. Then one meditates upon what one has understood. This is an extremely good way to proceed; however, it is not a very rapid way to proceed.

There are other methods of the Vajrayana that are not shared with the other vehicles. The Vajrayana involves a direct introduction to the reality of things. In the Vajrayana, one experiences, understands, and is introduced to the way in which all phenomena are self-risen and self-released. This is done in terms of meditative experience under the guidance of one's own particular root guru, whereby one is introduced to the wisdom that is to be realized. Having been introduced to that wisdom and relying upon it, one is able to abandon the kleshas or afflictions.

Various methods are taught within the tradition of the Vajrayana for recognizing and meditating in terms of the true nature of the mind. Such meditation serves as a way of abandoning various afflictions. However, it needs to be done properly, correctly, and genuinely. There are a variety of ways to go about it. For instance, there are the practices known as the *che-rim* or "stage of generation or creation" and there are also the practices of the *dzo-rim* or "stage of completion."

The methods of the creation stage make our mind extremely stable, vividly clear and bright, and this is done by meditating on the body of a deity. If we did not make use of this creation stage meditation but just went along casually with meditation, our mind would not become vivid and steady. In Tibet we have this way of meditating that involves the recitation of liturgies called sadhanas that make a great deal of noise when we do our practice. Those who have just entered into the practice of the Buddhadharma could very easily think that there is some discrepancy between the dharma that is taught in the books of the Buddhists and the sadhana or deity practice that is done in the Tibetan monastic institutions. For instance, one might feel that there is some discrepancy between the teachings saying that one ought to abandon the kleshas and Tibetans making a tremendous amount of chanting, ringing bells, banging cymbals, beating drums and so on. But, in fact, there is a very strong connection and purpose between those practices and the teaching about the eradication of the kleshas. By doing these sadhana practices, one's mind comes to an unwavering rest. In particular, when the mind is resting steadily and music is played, this serves as a method for the mind to rest even deeper than is possible in other methods. So, indeed, there is a real purpose and method to sadhana practice.

If we consider this in further detail, there are various elaborate arrangements made in deity practice which allow the mind to become steady, peaceful, and clear. In these practices there are the use of *tormas* which literally are "a scattered offering," but which are actually a figure made out of dough, usually barley in the Tibetan tradition. Those of you who have seen ceremonies of the Tibetan tradition have seen them painted with bright colors. However, someone new to this would look at these things and think, "What has that got to do with anything? How do these painted figures of dough serve to abandon kleshas? How do they serve to generate this very sharp knowledge, this very sharp knowing mind that is known as prajna?" Well, the purpose of these tormas or "painted dough figures" allows the mind to focus, to visualize and to observe the figure of a deity. The visualization of a deity is often very elaborate and if we just put a picture of the deity in front of the practitioner then it will be very easy for the practitioner to think, "Oh, I don't have to meditate. I don't have to visualize anything. There it is. I just have to look at it." But it is the conjunction between the torma and the visualized deity which enables us to heighten our mind and to rest in this.

When we first encounter strange religious objects or images we might think they serve no particular purpose. But if we analyze and investigate them more carefully, we will see that there is a real purpose for doing things in that particular way. In my own personal experience, when I had done some studying, but was new to liturgical ritual practices, I would look at these figures and think, "What is the point of that? It is not mentioned in any of the books I know about. There is nothing in the texts on Madhyamaka that speak about tormas. What is the point?" But actually, if you look carefully, you can begin to understand through your own knowledge and your own prajna the way these things are useful and important. They play an important role and aren't something one just does casually to amuse oneself. There is a real meaning to it; there is a purpose for it. When you understand that, then it is something you are delighted and cheered by and you like it quite a bit.

3. The Cessation of Suffering

The third noble truth is nirvana. From among effect and cause, this is an effect. This third noble truth is called the truth of cessation. In many Buddhist traditions cessation refers to the state of having abandoned the kleshas. In the texts on the Abhidharma, "individual, analytical cessations" are discussed in the sense that one needs to analyze carefully and thoroughly so that one is able to realize the true and actual nature of things. Having done this, then confusion and kleshas of all kind naturally cease. From that point of view, the cessation of suffering is the cessation of the kleshas.

Cessation is described as peaceful and auspicious. This means that one has separated from the kleshas, which make the mind disturbed and in a difficult situation, creating further obstructions and difficulties for oneself. Therefore, by being separated from those afflictions, one experiences peacefulness. This peacefulness is not a state that is a mere nothingness, rather, it is endowed with marvelous happiness or bliss. For that reason it is referred to as "auspicious or plentiful."

This peacefulness, which is one of the definitive marks of the truth of cessation, is also what is referred to as "definite emergence" which is sometimes translated as "renunciation." Literally this word means "definitely having arisen" in the sense that the happiness, pleasure, and the bliss of cessation is not a kind of happiness one finds in samsara, but rather it is a state of having achieved liberation and the final nirvana. In that way, this third noble truth, the truth of cessation, has these four characteristics: cessation, peacefulness, auspiciousness, and definite emergence.

The presentation of cessation according to the Mahayana generally refers to the kleshas that are to be abandoned. However, this does not mean that they have existed and later we have been able to abandon them, rather, it is a matter that we now recognize that the kleshas are not established in the true nature of the mind. Once we have thoroughly realized their lack of any existence in the nature of the mind, we naturally achieve their true cessation. In other words, we recognize that the afflictions or kleshas are naturally pacified. In the treatises of the Mahayana, it is said that all sentient beings possess Buddha essence and that the afflictions or kleshas are something that is only adventitious,[30] not in the actual nature of the mind. From that point of view, all sentient beings are primordially, right from the very start, a Buddha. However, the defilements, the kleshas, obstruct that Buddha nature, or Buddha essence. The consequence is that the qualities and enlightened activity are not manifest in those who still have such adventitious defilements. Nevertheless, because the defilements are extraneous, adventitious, and do not exist in the very nature of the mind, and the qualities of a Buddha (Buddha essence) are present in the mind right from the very beginning in all sentient beings, the defilements can be abandoned. Because it is possible to separate the kleshas from the inherent Buddha essence by realizing *dharmata* or true reality, we are able to abandon the defilements and achieve Buddhahood.

4. The Path

The fourth noble truth is called the truth of the path. There are two ways of translating this. In general, the path which is shared by all Buddhist traditions means achieving nirvana or Buddhahood. However we phrase it, nirvana or Buddhahood, it is necessary to achieve that effect or that truth, and in order to do so, one needs to exert oneself on the path, and thus it is said that the cessations are to be actualized. In order to actualize the cessations, one needs to rely upon the path in the stream of one's being.

The Five Paths

Whether we are speaking about the Hinayana or the Mahayana, the path is described by what are known as the five paths: accumulation, connection, seeing, meditation and no more learning.

We begin by entering the path of accumulation, which was described by the great master Vasubhandu as the need to engage in pure discipline, pure ethics, and to listen and contemplate deeply the meaning of the words of the Buddha and the words of the treatises written by the great learned scholars who commented and explained the Buddha's teachings. Having come to understand the meaning of these teachings, then one meditates upon the meaning that one has understood. Thus, this path of accumulation refers to the point of initially entering into the teachings.

In the second path of connection one meditates upon the meaning of the Buddha's teachings and develops the sign of having understood these teachings which is that the kleshas have diminished. At that point one has reached the path of connection, the second of the five paths.

It is called the path of connection because it connects one as an ordinary being to the ground of an arhat, a realized being. Those who are at the level of the path of connection are ordinary, common beings, however, this path of connection allows one to become an *arya* or noble being who has actually abandoned the afflictions.

The third path is the path of seeing. When one develops in one's own stream of being the authentic experience, one arrives at the point of the path of seeing, in which one sees the truth directly. Because one sees the truth correctly, this is called the path of seeing. In the context of the Hinayana, this is seeing the selflessness or egolessness of the person. In the context of the Mahayana, it is spoken of as seeing the true nature of dharmadhatu, the sphere of reality. Having seen that definitively, one abandons the emotional obstructions and obstructions of knowledge that are contradictory to that sphere of reality. One generates within oneself the wisdom of the path of seeing that abandons all obstructions which are to be abandoned on this path. When this is done, a great joy arises within oneself and, so this path of seeing, which is also the first bodhisattva level, is called the level of the "thoroughly joyful."

The fourth path is the path of meditation. On the path of seeing, we do indeed see the truth, but we do not achieve the fruition merely by having witnessed or seen it. Even though we have seen the truth of reality, nevertheless, there are still many latent predispositions that have been established in our stream of being. Due to our having become familiar to the kleshas from beginningless time, we are much more accustomed to confusion than to knowing the truth of reality. Therefore, to purify these latent dispositions, we need to grow familiar with the truth again and again and to extend that over a long period of time. This period of becoming familiar with the true nature of things is this fourth path of meditation. This fourth path abandons all of those predispositions that are to be abandoned on the path of meditation, and cultivates the appropriate wisdoms within the continuum of our being. In the context of the Hinayana, this period of practice is referred to as "returners," and "non-returners." In the Mahayana, this period of familiarization with reality on the path of meditation is called by the names of the second to the ten bodhisattva levels; from "stainless," to the "cloud of dharma."

Having traversed the various levels within the path of meditation we arrive at the fifth path called the path of no more learning. In the context of the Hinayana this is referred to as the "state of a foe-destroyer," or in Sanskrit *arhat*. In the context of the Mahayana, it refers to "the state of the genuinely, authentically, completely and perfectly enlightened Buddha." So that is the presentation of the five paths according to the shared or common tradition.

The Four Dharmas of Gampopa

The unshared or uncommon way of discussing the five paths in the Vajrayana tradition, and in particular in the Kagyu lineage of oral practice instructions given by Tilopa to Naropa, Naropa to Marpa, Marpa to Milarepa, Milarepa to Gampopa and so forth, it is as follows. Gampopa had a great deal to say about these things in his *Jewel Ornament of Liberation*. But this can be reduced to the Four Dharmas of Gampopa. These four dharmas or truths describe how the various wisdoms are generated within the stream of our being along the path.

I. May my mind become one with the dharma

The first dharma of Gampopa is "May my mind become one with the dharma." When we are attempting to enter into the practice of dharma, which is more important, the body, speech or mind? It is important that body and speech enter into the dharma, but this is not the most important thing. The most important thing is that our mind enters the dharma, therefore the first dharma of Gampopa is literally, "Mind goes into the dharma."

The way our mind can enter into the dharma is through the four thoughts that turn one's mind away from samsara which has been previously discussed. By understanding these four reminders we are able to enter into the dharma.

We then need to engage in a great deal of listening to the presentation of dharma and carefully contemplating its meaning. In the tradition set forth by the learned scholars or accomplished persons of Tibet, the treatises were mostly used for the study of the doctrine. Scholars from other countries look at this and consider this approach as mistaken. They say one should instead study the words of the Buddha directly; that if one is going to study the dharma one should focus upon the actual teachings of the Buddha. However, in the Tibetan tradition the study of the treatises is considered more valuable than the study of the actual words of the Buddha for the following reason. When the Buddha taught, he would teach different individuals on different occasions according to what they needed at that time, so the teachings were scattered, sort of piecemeal, here and there. The actual words of the Buddha are extremely vast and these words are not something that persons such as ourselves could easily engage in. Thus, the treatises by scholars following the Buddha gather together this vast collection of teachings and put them into a manageable, comprehensible form to clarify and illuminate aspects of the teachings that were not particularly clear.

Sometimes the Buddha spoke in a very terse, abbreviated way and it would be difficult to clearly understand the meaning given at that time. So the teachings in the treatises clarify such obscure teachings. Some of the main commentators were called the "Six Ornaments," these being the teachers Nagarjuna, Asanga, Gunaprabha, Aryadeva, Vasubhandu, and Sakyaprabha. They gathered together the teachings of the Buddha that had been scattered among many different texts, some which were very lengthy and they abbreviated them to cover their main point. They clarified their meaning which might be hidden and arranged the teachings so that one could understand their meaning. Having done this, it is now easy for a person to understand their meaning, easy to teach for those wishing to teach, and easy to train for those who wish to train in these teachings. Making the teachings more accessible was the purpose of arranging the teachings of the Buddha in these treatises or commentaries (*shastras* in Sanskrit). For example, with the Buddha's teachings in the *Prajnaparamita* ("Transcendent Wisdom"), there is a 100,000-stanza sutra that fills up twelve entire Tibetan volumes. Maitreya, through Asanga, summarized this sutra in a treatise known as *The Ornament of Clear Realization* (Skt. *Abhisamayalankara*) in just twenty chapters; so someone can now more easily read, study and focus upon this teaching.

Another example of one of the more concealed sutras on the teaching of emptiness is the *Prajnaparamita Sutra* which presents sixteen types of emptiness. Even though the sixteen emptinesses are taught in this sutra, the reasons for why there is a particular emptiness is not taught because on that occasion the Buddha taught highly developed bodhisattvas who themselves had profound realization, and so Buddha did not need to go about explaining the reason for these emptinesses in great detail. However, for ordinary beings like ourselves the great master Nagarjuna wrote treatises explaining emptiness, giving individual reasons for each emptiness. He explained the emptiness of phenomena with reasoning so that ordinary beings such as ourselves could develop a definitive knowledge and certainty about the meaning of emptiness.

So to summarize, the emphasis on the treatises is not from the viewpoint of saying that the words of the Buddha are of little importance, rather, it is from the viewpoint of making it possible to understand the meaning of the Buddha's words.

When it comes to actually practicing the dharma, the oral instructions are even more important than the treatises. This is because when we focus upon and study the treatises they do not tell us the way we should actually go about practicing. The manner of practice is not described clearly in the treatises, by saying, "First do this, and when you have done that, then do that." The treatises don't say, "If you have such and such an experience when you are practicing, then you should do such and such." For this reason, the various persons who achieved high meditative states have written treatises called "the oral instructions" explaining the way we should practice in accordance with the various sorts of experiences that masters have had. Thus the oral instructions say, "If you meet with this type of obstacle or have fallen into a certain type of state, then you would need to apply such and such a remedy." Explained in the oral instructions is the mode of practice appropriate for students. For that reason, when it comes to practice, the oral instructions are even more important than the treatises.

II. May Dharma progress along the path

The second dharma of Gampopa is "Dharma goes on the path." This refers mainly to the mind of enlightenment or bodhichitta. The root of bodhichitta is going for refuge in the Three Jewels with an attitude of respect and a knowledgeable confidence. In the tradition of the sutra one goes for refuge in the Three Jewels, which in Tibetan is literally "the Three Rare and Supreme Ones." The sutra tradition lists the Three Jewels as the Buddha, dharma and sangha. In the Vajrayana tradition we speak of going for refuge in the Three Jewels and the Three Roots. The Three Roots are the guru, the yidams, and the dharma protectors. The guru is the root of blessings, the yidams the root of siddhi (meditative accomplishment), and the dharma protectors the root of enlightened activity. So in the tradition of the Vajrayana one goes for refuge in the Three Jewels and the Three Roots.

Of the Three Roots, the guru is the root of blessings and is regarded as someone who is extremely important. If we were to think about this without preconceptions, we might look at a tradition that places a great emphasis on the guru as being faulty. If the guru occupies a place that is even more important than the Buddha himself, we would think that this is wrong because the Buddha is the source of this tradition. Why is it that the Buddha does not have the pre-eminent position; rather the guru occupies that place in the Vajrayana? However, there is no problem because, of course, the Buddha is someone whose good qualities were completely perceivable and extraordinary. He was highly elevated and an exalted person. However, the Buddha appeared in this world and passed away 2500 years and we do not have the good fortune of meeting the Buddha face to face. One might think that we are in an extremely poor situation of not having had the good fortune to meet with the Buddha in person. But in fact we aren't in such a situation. The truth of the matter is that we have the good fortune of experiencing no difference in our ability to hear the dharma as someone who heard the dharma from the Buddha directly. We have the good fortune of there being no difference between our situation and that of someone who heard the dharma from the Buddha himself because of the gurus of our lineage and our root guru. Because of the guru's instructions, we are able to practice the dharma and reach enlightenment. This comes about through the kindness of the root and lineage gurus. It is for this reason that we place such emphasis on the guru and regard him as the source of blessings.

The second root is the yidams or meditative deities, who are the source of accomplishment or siddhi. There are two types of siddhi: supreme siddhi and ordinary siddhi. The yidams are the source of siddhi because by practicing the dharma as taught by the Buddha, it is possible for us to achieve the final result of practice. However, the Buddha taught 84,000 types of dharma. Is it possible for us to practice all of these? No, that is not possible. Also is it not necessary for us to practice all of the dharmas that the Buddha taught. The reason the Buddha taught so many various dharmas was each was suitable to a particular student. However, the way we can practice all the teachings the Buddha gave is through the practice of the yidam, in particular, through the practice of *che-rim* or "generation stage of the yidam," and then through the practice of *dzo-rim* or "stage of completion of the yidam."[31] By doing this, we are able to practice everything that is essential in the entirety of the Buddha's teachings. For that reason, the yidam is said to be "the root of accomplishment, the root of siddhi and the very root of dharma."

The third root is the dharmapalas, the Sanskrit word for "protector of the dharma." They are the root of activity. Normally, we understand the third jewel to be the sangha, the spiritual community who are our companions and helpers on the path. They help to clear away situations that are obstacles to our progression along the path, and they increase all the conditions that help us progress along the path. However, there are situations in which they are not able to assist. Dharmapalas however, which can be Buddhas and bodhisattvas, can appear in other forms to clear away obstacles and support positive conditions. With that appearance, they clear away interruptions and obstacles that would keep us from progressing along the path and they provide favorable conditions that help us with our practice.

When it comes to practice, there are negative conditions that one must abandon and there are positive conditions that must be developed and increased. We must abandon all the ill deeds that we have accumulated or become accustomed to since beginningless time. The method for doing this is simply cutting and exposing it. In the tradition of Vajrayana, there is the practice of Vajrasattva or "vajra being." In this practice we visualize Vajrasattva above our head and through that are able to purify the ill deeds and obstructions that oppose our progress on the path.

To generate positive experience and realization within the stream of our being, we need to fulfill the concordant or positive conditions which are accumulating the collections of wisdom and merit. When we study the previous lives of the Buddha we find that in order to accumulate merit and wisdom he engaged in extraordinary generosity, such as giving his head, his limbs, whatever was necessary to sustain and benefit others. However, we are ordinary beings and it is not within our capacity to engage in that kind of generosity. However, there are profound methods that we can do, so that even though we are not able to engage in that kind of generosity, nevertheless, we are able to accumulate merit extensively. The profound method for this is offering our own wealth and resources mentally, by imagining that whatever we have, we offer it all to the enlightened and superior ones of the three times (past, present, and future) and all directions. In that way we are able to accumulate a vast amount of merit. This is the practice referred to as "offering of the mandala." In doing this practice we accumulate both wisdom and merit. Our wisdom increases to the extent that we can actually give rise to the profound experience of realization. So we accumulate the two collections without having to put forth an extraordinary exertion. We can manage this practice and accumulate these collections without huge exertion.

A further method for generating experience and realization within the continuum of one's being is the supplication to the Gurus of the Lineage, to one's Root Guru and the Lineage Gurus in the practice of "Guru Yoga," whereby we accumulate merit and wisdom. Thus, this is a third skillful method for dharma going along the path.

III. May the path clarify confusion
The third dharma of Gampopa says, "May the path clarify confusion" or "May the path disperse confusion." This refers to

the clearing away of the kleshas and the obstructions to knowledge. In the Vajrayana confusion is cleared away and destroyed by "the path of method" on the one hand and "the path of release" on the other. In this particular context, when we say the path of method, we are speaking about the Six Yogas of Naropa, and when we talk about the path of release, we are speaking about the practice of Mahamudra.[32] Individuals need to learn these two methods stage by stage based on their own experience, so that when the results of these practices arise, one has a genuine certainty and confidence in these practices and one develops a definite knowledge, ascertainment, and certainty about them.

IV. May confusion dawn as wisdom

The fourth dharma of Gampopa concerns "confusion dawning as wisdom." Having practiced on the path, confusion is clarified and wisdom or *yeshe* is generated within the continuum of one's being, it arises within one's being, and we have achieved actual Buddhahood. Thus, Gampopa spoke of confusion that we have dawning as wisdom.

QUESTIONS

Questions: Maybe you could tell us more about the dharmapalas? What kinds of things attract them to help you overcome obstacles? What methods invite and magnetize the dharmapalas?
Rinpoche: Mainly, the principal way one invites and magnetizes the assistance of the dharmapalas is through practicing the dharma properly and through caring for the welfare of other sentient beings. If one does so, then the dharmapalas will assist; if one does not, then they will not help. The background to this is that the Buddha made them into dharmapalas. In his presence, he said to them,

"Whoever practices the dharma properly and genuinely, please take care of that person as if he were my very own child, as if they were your very own child." Similarly, when one practices the dharma properly, then the dharmapalas, in accordance with the instruction of the Buddha, take care of us.

Question: *The fourth dharma of Gampopa says that wisdom dawns. How do the five wisdoms arise, the five aspects of that one wisdom arise out of the nature of the mind by seeing the nature of the mind?*
Rinpoche: The nature of our mind is dharmata and through realizing that, wisdom dawns within oneself. In particular, we speak about the transformation of the eight consciousnesses being transformed into the five wisdoms.

First of all, there are the five sensory consciousnesses based on the eye, ear, nose, tongue, and body sensations. When those five consciousnesses are transformed, they are transformed into the wisdom of accomplishing actions. This is the activity which accomplishes enlightened activity. Secondly, there is the sixth consciousness which is called "mental consciousness." Its function in the ordinary state is to recognize the details of things. When we have overcome our ignorance or delusion, this consciousness is transformed into the wisdom of individual realization, called "the wisdom of discriminating awareness." Thirdly, the seventh consciousness is called "afflicted consciousness." This consciousness in its state of ignorance or confusion is the belief that we have a solid and real self. When that confusion is dispelled, the afflictive mentality is transformed into the wisdom of equality. The eighth consciousnesses is usually called "the basis of all" or in Sanskrit the *alaya*. But this consciousness has two aspects. One aspect is just called the *alaya* or the basis of all, and the other aspect is called *alaya-vijnana*, "consciousness basis of all." When the basis of all is transformed, it becomes the mirror-like wisdom which knows all the varieties of phenomena. Mirror-like wisdom is the Buddha's omniscient wisdom which realizes each and every phenomenon, or we could say, everything that exists just as it is. The consciousness basis of all (alaya-vijnana), when transformed, becomes the wisdom of dharmadhatu, the wisdom of the sphere of reality. It realizes reality; it realizes the mode, manner, nature of things, how they are.

Chapter 11

KUSHINAGAR AND IMPERMANENCE

Since the motivation is extremely important and is the principal thing when listening to the dharma, as we begin this teaching please turn your mind towards supreme enlightenment for the sake of all sentient beings, thus arousing bodhichitta.

The place where the Buddha himself passed beyond suffering or entered nirvana is known as Kushinagar in Sanskrit. The Tibetan name means "the city of the supreme type of grass, kusha-grass," so it is Kushinagar in Sanskrit.

The Benefits of Developing a Discriminating Awareness of Impermanence

Generally speaking, when the Buddha came to Kushinagar, he taught both the shorter sutra on nirvana and the longer sutra on nirvana, the *Mahaparanirvana Sutra*. He passed into nirvana; passing beyond all suffering. Of the various deeds of the Buddha, his passing into nirvana taught mainly on impermanence. One might think, "Although everything else is impermanent, the Buddha himself is permanent." But when even the Buddha dies, passes into nirvana and shows impermanence in that way, then one cannot help but realize that all things are impermanent in a very profound way.

The Buddha said that of the different kinds of discriminating awareness, the supreme discriminating awareness is the thought of impermanence. He then gave three reasons to explain this.

First, in the beginning, the discriminating awareness of impermanence exhorts one toward the dharma. One usually does not wish to practice the dharma when one begins, one does not have faith in the dharma, however, through developing discriminating awareness of impermanence, one develops the wish to enter into the dharma and to practice it which leads to faith and longing in the dharma. So, in the beginning, the discriminating awareness that things are impermanent arouses one to enter into the dharma.

Second, in the intermediate phase, the awareness of impermanence stimulates great exertion. One might not think that the practice of the dharma is anything of particularly great importance. After entering into the dharma, one might not have been able to develop great exertion to practice. However, through awareness of impermanence one is able to exert oneself greatly. With an awareness of impermanence, exertion to practice can be generated and if one becomes lazy, one can abandon that laziness. Thus, in the intermediate phase, the discriminating awareness of impermanence enables one to exert oneself strongly.

If we think about this from the viewpoint of our own experience we can understand that this is true. Examining those who have entered into the path of the dharma, we see that most of them came to it with quite a clear understanding of impermanence. Some people initially enter the dharma solely through an understanding of impermanence. Therefore, the recognition of impermanence is said to be a condition that exhorts us towards entering into the dharma. Frequently there are people who have entered into the dharma in a very direct way, nevertheless, they don't seem to have the leisure to practice the dharma because of being distracted by many worldly activities. They ask, "What remedy is there for this?" I answer that the Buddha said that the remedy for this is to remember impermanence. If one remembers impermanence and truly takes it to mind, then one will be able to exert oneself strongly. If one is not able to meditate, then through being mindful of impermanence one will be able to meditate. If one is doing the preliminary practices of Ngöndro and does not have much success with doing prostrations or reciting the 100-syllable mantra of Vajrasattva, if one remembers impermanence, then this will enable one to give birth to proper exertion.

The contemplation on impermanence does not depend solely upon what we have heard from our guru or read in a book. By looking carefully at the world we can understand the teaching of impermanence. Just looking around at our worldly affairs we understand impermanence. Studying the lives of our family members we will recognize impermanence. Looking at the change in our own body, speech, and mind will cause us to understand impermanence. Studying the fortunes of other people such as the length of life, and how life goes for them, can teach us about impermanence. Life itself gives us an introduction to impermanence. So, if we look carefully, look at the details of things, we will understand this teaching of impermanence. After seeing this we will understand the necessity of practicing the dharma and the benefit of practicing the dharma, and we will see the disadvantageous events of not practicing the dharma.

If we look at the impermanence of the world we might think, "Well, so what? There is no particular fault to that." In particular, if we look at the life span of animals, whether their life was permanent or impermanent, does it really make much of a difference? Would there be any great advantage to it being permanent? No, it doesn't really matter in their case. However, in our case, having a life as a human being; of being free and well favored, of having the seed of prajna within ourselves, of having intelligence that can be increased greatly, it does make a great deal of difference to recognize that life is impermanent. If we are able to recognize that and exert ourselves in the practice of the dharma, then there will be great benefit for ourselves and for others. By recognizing impermanence and practicing the dharma our ability to benefit others will increase in the future and the capacity to be of service will increase. Since we now have this opportunity and good fortune it would be a shame to waste it. So as not to waste it, it is important to take this teaching, this fact of impermanence, which helps us to realize that having this fortunate life is not something minor, but rather it is something of real meaning. Through recognizing that, we are able to undertake the activity of the dharma with real exertion.

The third benefit of developing a discriminating awareness of impermanence is that it serves as the companion and aid for the fruition of our practice. In the beginning, the awareness of impermanence exhorts us to the dharma. In the intermediate phase, the awareness of impermanence enables us to give birth to great exertion. Having practiced the dharma, the recognition of impermanence allows us to achieve complete and genuine enlightenment.

Questions

Question: I believe that Buddha said that after his death there would be 500-year periods of decline in Buddhism and I believe we are at the end of the fifth period of 500 years. Does Buddhism still have a chance in this world? Are Buddhism and the people practicing it impermanent? Will that decline as well?"

Rinpoche: The Buddha said that there would be ten 500-year stages in the history of the dharma. He indicated a steady decline. In one stage there would be people who actually achieve the effect (enlightenment), and later they wouldn't achieve the effect, but there would still be practice. Later they wouldn't practice but there would still be the scriptural tradition. Later on there wouldn't even be a scriptural tradition, but still signs of the tradition.

When the Buddha said these things he was taking the perspective of the overall increase and decrease of dharma in the whole world. He wasn't talking about the situation of individual persons. Whether the dharma is flourishing widely or whether it is not flourishing widely in the world, the excellent dharma is still the excellent dharma. If one has the good fortune to meet with it and to practice it, the fact that it has not spread so widely in the world does not present an obstacle for oneself. There is no particular reason why one could not practice and achieve the complete fruition. Whether you are at the very first of these 500-year stages or the very last of those 500-year stages, when you yourself meet with the dharma, then you have the opportunity to practice. It is not the case that you wouldn't be able to achieve the complete fruition of practice when you meet the dharma. What one accomplishes is dependent simply upon oneself. It leads back to oneself, whether the dharma has spread widely in the world or not.

If we were to consider this from an example of a sweet fruit, it might be that in one part of the world it was quite plentiful and in another part it didn't exist. But even if you were in a place where that fruit was very rare and not many people could enjoy it, if you happened to get one, there is no reason why you would not find it delicious and nourishing. You could enjoy it just as much as anybody anywhere else could. So, when you meet with the dharma, it is completely available to you. When you leave here and go back to your home and are able to exert yourself at practice, if you are able to practice well, that will be great. There is no reason at all for you to think that because the dharma declined at this point in the history you can't accomplish fruition.

There is no need for us to have any doubt about our opportunity to achieve the fruition of the dharma. We could consider this in the light of the prophecy Naropa gave to Marpa. He said that the history of this lineage would be one in which each successive generation of students would be even higher than its predecessors. Having Milarepa in mind, Naropa told Marpa that he would have a student who would be a marvelous, fantastic student, that Marpa would be very delighted in this student and that because of this student the lineage would flourish. It came about in just that way. In the same way, Milarepa had a fantastic student, Gampopa, and I think he was extremely delighted and well pleased. That was the history of the lineage in that each successive generation of the upholders of the lineage were fantastic students, who became completely accomplished. Things have become better and better and more and more profound. From that point of view, there is no reason for anybody to think they cannot accomplish the fruition of the dharma.

Same student: I want to confess that I asked His Holiness the Karmapa the same question 11 years ago. He said, "Yes, it is true that we are in a state of decline." I don't know which tantra he was quoting, but he said, "In the tantras this is when Vajrayana will flourish as well." This was his reply.

Question: Rinpoche, when we were at Sarnath, we were talking about the truth of the path. At that time you were talking about the path of connection to the way of superior beings, when one generates within one's own continuum a genuine experience and one sees genuinely. Would you please expand on that?

Rinpoche: The path of connection has four aspects: (1) heat, (2) peak, (3) forbearance, and (4) supreme quality.

(1) By practicing and cultivating the first of the five paths, the path of accumulation, the sign of having completed the path of accumulation is called "heat" because the first of the four levels of the path of connection is called "the heat path of connection."

(2) Next, one has the sign of experiences increasing. They rise to a pinnacle. From that point of view, the second of the four levels of the path is called "the peak of the path of preparation."

(3) As one's practice continues, one develops such forbearance that afflictions and obstacles cannot remain. So the third level of this path of connection is called "forbearance."

(4) One then passes to the fourth level, which is called "supreme worldly quality." It is given that name because there is no path of a worldly being superior to that path. For that reason, it is called supreme worldly quality.

All four of these are done mainly in terms of one's knowledge, confidence and practice. They then connect one to seeing dharmata or reality directly. That seeing reality directly is called "the path of seeing" and one achieves the ground of an arhat.

Question: *I wondered if you could say something about the way in which bodhisattvas perceive relative or conventional truth (Tib. kun-zop? There seem to be a number of stages. One way, there is a manifestation and finally the Buddha sees all conventional things directly.*

Rinpoche: Generally speaking, when one talks about conventional or relative phenomena, one is talking about the way in which things appear. When one is talking about ultimate truth (Tib. *dön-dam*), one is talking about the way things actually are and thus about emptiness. We are speaking in the context of the Middle-way School, the Madhyamaka.

The appearance of phenomena is a union of *kun-zop* and *dön-dam*, a union of the conventional and the ultimate reality. These two truths or types of phenomena are not contradictory to one another and do not obstruct each other. When we talk about objects of perception, the conventional and the ultimate truth are not contrary to one another but both exist right within that object. When objects appear on the conventional level, at that very time their nature is emptiness on the ultimate level. These two are not in any way contrary to one another. If we speak about the object from the viewpoint of the dualistic consciousness, there is an obstacle to seeing the object on both the conventional and the ultimate level. The ultimate emptiness is the object perceived with superior wisdom. The conventional appearance is the perception of the object based on confusion or incorrect wisdom. So, there is a difficulty in seeing the ultimate and conventional level at the same time because they appear to different types of consciousnesses. But that is not to say that they are in and of themselves contrary to one another. They are not contrary in that these obstructions to our perception do not exist with the object itself.

Conventional phenomena appear to ordinary beings and, when these conventional objects appear, ordinary beings are not able to realize their ultimate nature, which is called the dharmata. When one sees dharmata (reality, the truth) directly, then conventional phenomena do not appear. The emptiness is realized when conventional phenomena have been abandoned, so to speak. This realization is called "meditative equipoise," *nam-jag* in Tibetan; it means something like "the mind being set evenly or equally." However, when one rises from that meditative equipoise, mistaken appearances again arise in one's perception because one has accumulated predispositions for the appearance of objects from beginningless time. Although one has realized the ultimate once, one has not abandoned all of those latent predispositions for the conventional appearance of phenomena that exist in our mind. Thus, when one rises out of meditative equipoise into post-meditation, phenomena appear again.

After bodhisattvas realize dharmata directly, then when they perceive conventional phenomena in post-meditation, do the perceptions of bodhisattvas differ from those who have not realized dharmata? Yes, their perception is different because ordinary beings take all these conventional appearances to be true, real things, whereas those who have realized dharmata directly understand that phenomena are like an illusion, a dream. So, bodhisattvas experience of phenomena is different from that of an ordinary person. Realizing dharmata then is the beginning of the first bodhisattva level, called the "thoroughly joyful." The bodhisattva continues with this realization and gradually his or her latent predispositions are purified with there being fewer and fewer of them until the eighth bodhisattva level is reached when the predispositions have been almost completely purified and abandoned. Even though the bodhisattva has purified these predispositions, they still understand the appearances of conventional phenomena. The way in which they know the appearance of conventional phenomena when arriving at a very high level is not through their own appearances of objects but rather from knowing them in the way they appear to other sentient beings. This wisdom is fully developed and is known as "the wisdom that knows the variety of phenomena," which is one of the two aspects of a Buddha's wisdom. So, the bodhisattva knows phenomena as they appear to others rather than as something arising from their own perspective. They are no longer subject to ignorance and thus they do not have the sort of appearance and experience that comes about through the power of ignorance.

Finally, at the level of a Buddha, there is no division between meditation and post-meditation, rather at all times the Buddha realizes both the wisdom of variety of conventional phenomena and the wisdom of ultimate phenomena which is their emptiness. A Buddha is not obstructed from realizing these two wisdoms and not subject to the confusion to which ordinary beings possess.

Question: On the Vajrayana path, when the mind is resting in that equipoise state, one arises from meditation and phenomena dawn. How should one view the dawning of phenomena at the end of the session?
Rinpoche: Generally speaking, there is just the natural arising and appearance of phenomena. If one's experience and realization go well, then one will be free from attachment and clinging to those appearances that just naturally arise. On the other hand, if one does not have particularly good experience and realization, then one will have attachment and clinging to things just as

ordinary people do. In particular, if one is doing intensive practice within a retreat situation, for instance, when one arises from a session, rather than having discriminating awareness of phenomena as common things, one should have the discriminating awareness of oneself as a deity, of one's environment as the retinue, and so forth. This is to view phenomena as illusions or as dreams, and one should put some energy into having very careful mindfulness of these experiences.

Chapter 12

LUMBINI AND THE EXCELLENT DHARMA

THE THREE PRINCIPLES OF THE EXCELLENT DHARMA

The reason we go on pilgrimage is that we wish to become mindful of and think about the exalted activity of the Buddha. The Buddha engaged in meaningful and wonderful activities of taking birth in this world, achieving enlightenment, turning the wheel of dharma, and passing into nirvana. Our purpose of going on pilgrimage is thinking about what the Buddha did. A pilgrimage is not just a worldly activity; we are speaking about the good qualities of the Buddha's body, speech, and mind which are unsurpassed by other teachers and that is because the Buddha taught the genuine path that leads to liberation.

The Buddha said to his students, "I am teaching you the means to become liberated from samsara." Further, he said, "Whether or not you achieve liberation depends only upon you. So make the effort." That is to say, the achievement of liberation does not depend upon the Buddha, rather it is through practicing and following the way he taught that we can achieve liberation. If we do this, then we can achieve liberation. There is no reason for us to think that we would not be able to do so. If, on the other hand, we do not practice the teachings of the Buddha, we will not achieve liberation. So our achievement of liberation or our failure to do so depends only upon ourselves.

So we can practice and achieve liberation because the Buddha taught the paths that lead to liberation. These paths are called the excellent dharma. When we make supplications, we say "the unsurpassable protection is the excellent dharma." This is to say that the excellent dharma actually protects us from suffering. It is the dharma that we need to practice. The dharma that was taught by the Buddha was extremely vast and it is said there are 84,000 different dharmas. However, Buddha also abbreviated this path very precisely as three principles of (1) not engaging in harmful activity, (2) engaging in beneficial activity, and (3) thoroughly taming the mind.

This first means to not perform ill or negative deeds. This means not engaging in activities that are harmful to oneself or harmful to others such as killing, stealing, lying, or any of the injurious and non-beneficial activities of body and speech that can cause one to accumulate bad actions or negative karma.

The second principle is to engage in marvelous activity or virtue such as generosity, discipline, and ethics. In that way, one enters into the activity that accumulates the roots of virtue.

The main method whereby one could practice these first two points of not engaging in harmful activity and engaging in beneficial activity leads mainly back to one's own mind. So the third essential point that the Buddha taught was to thoroughly tame your mind. These three main principles are the Buddha's own condensation of the dharma into its very essence. Those are the paths that he taught. In this third principle of taming one's own mind, all of us without exception have minds that are covered over by the fault of afflictions, the kleshas. And these kleshas can be extremely powerful, therefore, we need to engage in the methods for pacifying the afflictions.

When I was teaching at Sarnath on the topic of the four truths and I reached the topic of the truth of the paths, I indicated that there were four different points that I wanted to cover, but I only got to three of them because we ran out of time. I talked about the methods for abandoning the kleshas through the practice of the Hinayana, the Mahayana and the Vajrayana. I did not reach the topic of how one suppresses them. I want to talk about that now because I think it is an important topic. All of us, whether we have the difficulty and hardship of desire, hatred, pride, and so forth. If we can abandon them, if we can diminish them, suppress them, it is very helpful.

Abandoning the Afflictions

Taking the example of hatred, we find people don't like to be angry and full of hate, nevertheless, they naturally and helplessly fall into it. And yet, when we become hateful and angry, the effect is not helpful or beneficial for either ourselves or others. We understand that, but without having the independent will to do otherwise, in certain situations we fall under the sway of anger. Many people look for a method that would enable them to deal effectively with anger and hatred. For instance, sometimes in some of the disciplines of psychology they may suggest one should act it out. So we take a stick and beat up a pillow or something like that. They might also say that if you were to just prevent the hatred, it would create a mental and emotional problem for you. Generally speaking, what they are saying is good but it is not a very skilled method to deal with anger.

In the Buddhist way we have methods for setting the afflictions aside with force, without having come to the point of exhibiting them. This is done by acting on the very root of the afflictions, which is by realizing selflessness. For instance, Shantideva in *The Way of the Bodhisattva* said, "One should recognize afflictions and faults as faults. One needs to see accurately that the afflictions cause problems for us. If we think that afflictions have good qualities and are beneficial, then we will not be able to abandon them. But if we understand that the afflictions are harmful to us, we will recognize them as our real foe." Our normal thinking when things go wrong is to think most of the time that somebody else is causing obstacles for us and consequently think that that person is our enemy or someone we don't like. As a result, we get angry at that person. When we begin to hate that person, we actually harm him or her and ourselves also. The truth of the matter is that it is the kleshas or afflictions that are harmful and, the harm that it does is extensive and lasts for a long time. That is the situation that has to be clearly seen.

Why the Afflictions Cause Long-Lasting Harm

Let us speak a little more extensively about what it means to say that the harm done by the afflictions is both extensive and long-lasting.

First of all, if we are harmed by another person, then the harm that person does to oneself can last for a period of some years. The harm that is done to oneself by the afflictions is that they have kept us in the suffering of cyclic existence; they have bound us in samsara up to this moment and the afflictions will keep us in samsara forever, until one gets rid of these afflictions. Furthermore, by acting on the afflictions they throw us into the lower realms where we have to undergo all kinds of suffering for a long period of time. If we consider the harm done by the afflictions in terms of their extent and compare that to the harm done by an external person, then the most a person we perceive as our enemy can do is to do harm to our possessions, our bodies, and possibly our lives. Enemies can only do that once, that is, for just one lifetime. However, the harm done by the afflictions throws us into painful and difficult lifetimes such as the hell realms and other lower realms. The suffering that we undergo in these realms is inconceivable. So, if we consider things from this perspective, we can see that it is the afflictions which are our real enemies. In other words, our actual foes reside right within our own mind.

Let us consider the contrast between a person whom we take as our enemy and our afflictions. Which one are we going to take as a friend and which one are we going to take as an enemy? If another person harms us and we go home and practice patience, and we bear that suffering and don't harm that person in return, rather we benefit that person by helping them, then later our foe may well become our friend. Someone who harmed us becomes someone who helps us. If, on the other hand, we treat our afflictions with the same sort of affection, no matter what we do for them, they will never become our real benefactor, rather, they become stronger and stronger; something that works against our own purpose and practice.

Similarly, if we succeed in returning harm to somebody who has harmed us and we steal everything they have and banish that person to another land, then later when they have recovered from the wound we have inflicted and their power has increased again, they will come back with renewed force. If we kill one enemy, then that does not solve the problem either because that person's relatives and friends will gather together and come against us. Eventually, no matter how much harm we do to an enemy, they regain their capacity and they come back to harm us again. The afflictions are not like that. If you actually abandon the afflictions by taming your mind, they are naturally pacified and pass away. The afflictions don't come back again to do harm once you have tamed your mind. The afflictions don't have the capacity to gather friends, relatives and allies and seek revenge. When you have tamed your mind, then you have tamed your mind.

So, in brief, we need to recognize that the afflictions are harmful to us and others and that they are a fault. The afflictions do not bring benefit to us, and if we can abandon them by taming our mind, then we can be free from them altogether and forever. In contrast, by relying on the afflictions the only thing that comes out of this is hardship and suffering. If we understand that and contemplate that again and again, we will be able to diminish the afflictions.

There are two different ways to deal with the afflictions. One is to tear them out from the root so that they are gone forever. The other is apply temporary antidotes, so that one is not able to uproot them altogether, rather, one engages in the methods simply to reduce the force of the afflictions. What I am talking about here are the methods to reduce the force of the afflictions rather than what was previously discussed as the methods for uprooting the afflictions permanently and forever by realizing selflessness.

The Four Immeasurables

I have discussed various methods to diminish the force of afflictions presented in Shantideva's *The Bodhisattva Way of Life*. It is also important to turn one's mind toward the good, helpful, and pure way of thinking and then to increase whatever good thoughts one has. In the Vajrayana there is a way for increasing whatever good thoughts one has by practicing what is known as "the four immeasurables." This practice of the four immeasurables is common to all the traditions of Buddhist meditation. If we are going to talk about the practice of the four immeasurables, let us consider first of all the way in which one cultivates love and compassion, which is the antidote to their opposite, hatred.

Love and compassion

Generally, all religious traditions recommend an attitude of love and compassion. All of them regard this as important. However, in the Buddhist tradition there is a way of cultivating and developing love and compassion that is different from many religions. If we practice love and compassion without the particular feature that is distinctive to the Buddhist tradition that is not bad. In the Buddhist tradition, it is said that there is no one who is utterly without love and compassion. The Buddha expressed this by saying, "All sentient beings have the sugatagarbha, 'the essence of the one gone to bliss.'" Even though all sentient beings do have this sugata-essence, not everyone has limitless compassion that is taught in the Buddhist tradition. The way in which one develops love and compassion limitlessly is through contemplative meditative practice, and this distinctive Buddhist method is extremely important.

What then is limitless love and compassion? One may have love and compassion for one's own son and daughter but not for others, or perhaps one may have love and compassion for those who are of one's race or caste or social class and not for others. One might have love and compassion for everybody who belongs to one's country but not for those of certain other countries. Some people have love and compassion for animals but not for humans. Some people have love and compassion for humans but not for animals. Generally speaking, when one's love and compassion is for one class of sentient beings but not for another, then that love and compassion is mixed with attachment, with you having a harmful attitude toward those for whom you don't like, and you often wish that suffering comes to them. Although it is good to have partial love and compassion that extends to one and not the other, the nature of this love and compassion is not terribly beneficial. In fact, it brings harm to both oneself and others.

The distinctive feature of love and compassion as taught in the Buddhist tradition is the feature of limitlessness. When we make a division between those for whom we love and have compassion and those for whom we don't like, then we have made a limit to our compassion. In partial compassion we have drawn a line between those we like and those we don't. If we have compassion for humans but not for animals, then we have limited how much love and compassion we are going to have. This kind of love and compassion is not fully endowed love and compassion. That is why the Buddha called true or full love and compassion "immeasurable." So the love and compassion taught in the Buddhist tradition doesn't have the fault of benefiting one person or group and implicitly harming those outside the group. Rather, as Buddhists we seek to benefit all and harm no one. From that point of view it is called immeasurable. Thus, immeasurable love and compassion are very important.

Equanimity

We have been speaking about love and compassion as part of the four immeasurables. We have spoken about love and compassion first of all, which generally is the order of how these immeasurables are arranged. However, the method of practicing and developing the four immeasurables as explained in the oral instructions does not begin with love and compassion but rather with cultivating equanimity. The reason for that is that if we do not begin by cultivating equanimity, then we will not be able to extend love and compassion to all sentient beings. Rather, it is said that if one starts out with love for one's friends and rejects those who are one's enemies, then if one increases the force of the love one has, the hatred for one's enemies will remain. So you have to begin by developing a loving ground with an equal attitude towards everyone. Having an attitude of equanimity towards all sentient beings means you are free of attachment to one and rejection of others, so that one's mind settles down, is sort of comfortable, relaxed, not tight, but free of attachment, free of rejection, sort of subtle, calm and spacious.

Love

Having become accustomed to equanimity, we begin to develop love for others. Love is the wish that others have happiness, and we wish that those who do not have happiness will achieve it. The unusual way we cultivate love in the Buddhist tradition is that we not only wish that others have happiness but also that they develop the causes of happiness. If we were to think about helping others attain happiness, we have to realize that we don't have the ability to do that and that that they would still suffer. There are all sorts of different kinds of happiness that we wish to have and all sorts of different kinds of suffering from which we wish to be free from. Everyone wants to eliminate their suffering of body and their suffering of mind. But simply wishing that we are free from physical or mental suffering doesn't eliminate the suffering. We need to work on the causes of happiness and we need to separate ourselves from the causes of suffering to have true, lasting happiness. What are the causes of happiness? Pure thoughts and exerting ourselves in spiritual practice that is beneficial and virtuous. If we do that, then happiness will be achieved naturally. Therefore, what we need in particular is to work on the causes of happiness.

Compassion

Similarly, when we begin to cultivate compassion for others, that is, wishing that others be free of suffering, we need to cultivate the wish that others will not only be free of suffering but that they will be freed from the causes of suffering. The causes of suffering are actions that are not beneficial, non-virtuous actions, ill deeds, and afflictions. Thus, compassion has the aspect of the wish that all sentient beings be free of suffering and its causes.

The main feature of love is wishing that others have happiness and the main feature of compassion is wishing that they be free of suffering. That of course is the case, but when it comes to practice, it is not the case that we can directly give them happiness and they will immediately be free of suffering. In order for that to come about we need to work on the causes of happiness and we need to be freed from the causes of suffering. Therefore, when it comes down to practicing love and compassion, what is important is working on the causes of having happiness and at the causes of being free of suffering.

Joy

Generally speaking, when we see someone who is suffering we feel compassion and somewhat discouraged. This experience occurs because we realize that we cannot actually do much for them. We would like to free them from suffering, we would like to give them a happy situation but we are not able to do so and, therefore, we feel somewhat discouraged. This might lead us to think that compassion is itself a type of suffering. However, the Buddha said that love and compassion here is not just a painful state of mind, because even though we realize that we are not able to give others a state of being free from suffering right away, we can take heart that we can help them in the practice of the causes of happiness and help them abandon the causes of suffering. So, from that point of view we are tremendously encouraged, we feel heartened. Therefore, the effect of limitless love and compassion results in what is referred to as "measureless joy." This is the measureless joy of knowing that we can help others achieve happiness and to become free of suffering. Helping them begin the practices of accumulating the causes of happiness and abandoning the causes of suffering results in measureless compassion, measureless love, and measureless joy.

Sometimes people say to me that bodhisattvas must have inconceivable and measureless suffering. Since they see all the suffering that sentient beings have and since the suffering is measureless, the suffering of bodhisattvas must also be inconceivable. Actually it is not that way because when a bodhisattva sees someone suffering, he or she knows that he or she possesses the resources to separate that person from suffering and help them to achieve happiness. A bodhisattva knows that there are methods to free other people from suffering. So knowing that he or she can eliminate another person's suffering, a bodhisattva feels extremely joyful. From that point of view, rather than having measureless suffering, a bodhisattva has measureless joy.

Those then are the practices of the four immeasurables. We could say that equanimity is a preliminary practice of the four immeasurables, that love and compassion are the main body of the practice and, that joy is the fruition of the practice of the four immeasurables.

Bodhichitta

There is a particular feature that is lacking within love and compassion that we have not discussed so far, and that is prajna, a very clear and sharp knowledge that is a characteristic of bodhichitta or in English, the mind of enlightenment. This is to say, the love and compassion discussed thus far is concerned only with temporary happiness and not with final happiness. We wish to benefit others, but that only lasts so long if the mind of enlightenment, bodhichitta, the way to establish all sentient beings in enlightenment, is not included. Without bodhichitta forming one's practice of the four immeasurables, the benefit can only last for a temporary period; not something that would go from lifetime to lifetime. What we really would like to do is to transform others so that they need not undergo suffering at all and have happiness lifetime after lifetime. But happiness of that kind is the attainment of actual Buddhahood. So we join these four immeasurables with the practice of bodhichitta, which allows people to reach complete liberation so that they will not have to experience any kind of suffering ever again.

When the four immeasurables have been conjoined with prajna or "intelligence," then they become bodhichitta.

QUESTIONS

Question: *You said that the afflictions do not have the power of being friends and do not gather together to attack you in revenge. What about the maras?*
Rinpoche: The story of the Buddha is a symbolic representation. The attack of the maras was not an attack of the Buddha's afflictions. It actually referred to demonic beings who, seeing that the Buddha was about to achieve enlightenment and achieve the means for establishing innumerable sentient beings in liberation and enlightenment, didn't like it and attacked Buddha in a display of warfare.

Question: *Does that mean that in our personal path of trying to attain enlightenment, struggling to attain liberation, the maras are going to attack us in different ways?*
Rinpoche: For the time being we need not worry about it. Should it happen that we reach the point of being about to achieve enlightenment, we will be able to deal with it. It is just to say, the Buddha established a limitless number of maras on the path of liberation and omniscience. He tamed even malicious beings and put them on the path leading to liberation and enlightenment. In particular, he tamed the very kings and rulers of the families of these demonic beings, the very lords of the world, and led them onto the path of the dharma. What was left for their followers was to do similarly.

That was the story of the Buddha. For our own situation, we are not people who have great capacity. The maras were upset by the fact that someone was about to achieve great capacity. We are not people who have arrived at that level and, therefore, we are not people who are going to arouse that sort of opposition from demonic forces in the universe. When we reach the point of being about to achieve enlightenment, then we will have the power to deal with such demonic forces.

Question: Maybe it is not maras that we run up against, maybe it is something less powerful, but it does seem that there is a sense of overcoming obstacles that occur on the path.
Rinpoche: Yes, we have obstacles. If one is able to reduce the force of one's own internal afflictions, then external agents such as demonic beings will not be able to harm one very much.

Question: Sometimes one simply feels ill at ease and is not quite sure what it is all about, this feeling of discomfort and unhappiness, not quite sure whether it is anger or desire. What can we do to clarify that and to see what is actually going on?
Rinpoche: At that time it will not help a great deal to look outside, trying to figure out something based upon the external. What will help is simply to look within one's own mind; look inside and carefully and slowly contemplate, seeing what is in one's mind. Then it will become clear.

Question: I was wondering how a bodhisattva feels when he sees suffering and that such a person cannot open himself for the dharma, so he cannot do anything to help?
Rinpoche: A bodhisattva's joy does not depend upon one individual person; his or her perspective is to consider all sentient beings throughout all of space. Even if at that particular time a bodhisattva is not able to help a particular sentient being achieve happiness and freedom from suffering, he or she would not become discouraged and feel disheartened. A bodhisattva has a much wider and longer-term view of things. Right now may not be the

appropriate time for that particular person to be tamed by the dharma, however, there will be a time in the future when that person can be tamed by the dharma. In the meantime, there are a limitless number of sentient beings the bodhisattva can help now by showing them the path to liberation. In the future there will be a time when the person who is not presently to be tamed by the dharma can be tamed by the dharma.

Question: There is a very important verse in the Madyhamakavatara, *which states: "Compassion is the cause of bodhisattvas," and, I think, "bodhisattvas are the cause of becoming a Buddha." You talked about the last point when you said that you need to connect love and compassion with prajna. I wonder if you would expand on that?*
Rinpoche: I think indeed there is a relationship between the point I was trying to make about bringing that kind of perspective into one's practice of the four immeasurables, bringing that kind of prajna to the four immeasurables, and the very nature of bodhichitta. In the opening verse of Chandrakirti's *Madyhamakavatara*, it says, "the union of compassion and a non-dual mind is the cause of the Buddhas' offspring," with "offspring" being an epithet for bodhisattvas. What is being spoken about in that verse is, first of all, compassion. And secondly, when it speaks of non-dual awareness or non-dual mind, it refers to prajna. When one first achieves those together and directs them toward the achievement of enlightenment, then that is bodhichitta itself. Bodhichitta is the actual cause of achieving Buddhahood. So I think that what I was trying to say and the meaning of the verse from the *Madyhamakavatara* are the same.

Question: From the perspective of the time-scale and the breadth and vision of a bodhisattva, those beings who are not ripe to enter the dharma at this time but in some future time, and undergoing degrees of greater or lesser suffering until that time, can that suffering then be looked upon from the viewpoint of that bodhisattva's time-scale, depth and vision? Could this suffering be viewed so as to enter into the dharma?

Rinpoche: Yes, I think that what you described is indeed the case. In particular, there is a verse from Shantideva in the *Bodhisattva's Way of Life* where it says, "Even if you are someone who harms a bodhisattva, you will achieve enlightenment as a result of that." This is to say, although someone might actually inflict injury on a bodhisattva, because of that bodhisattva's aspiration prayers and vision, that action of harming a bodhisattva is actually establishing the relationship that eventually, in the end, that person who harmed the bodhisattva will enter into the practice of dharma. From the longer perspective, it establishes the possibility for that person to enter the dharma, to practice the dharma and to achieve the fruition of the dharma.

Question: What does it mean to say that a bodhisattva is a son of the Buddha and how does that fit with Rinpoche saying that there are other causes?

Rinpoche: When we talk about a bodhisattva being the child or son of Buddhas, we have to make a distinction between what we refer to as the cause of a bodhisattva and secondary factors which we call conditions. For instance, if we are talking about planting a sprout, what is the cause of that sprout? The seed is the cause of the sprout and secondary factors such as water, fertilizer and the sun are conditions that contribute to the growth of the plant.

Similarly, if we apply the same analogy to a bodhisattva, then compassion, love and prajna are like the seed; they are the causes of a bodhisattva in that it is through a compassionate, non-dual mind, and the aspiration for enlightenment for the sake of all sentient beings, that one becomes a bodhisattva and then a Buddha. If we were to talk about the secondary factors of a bodhisattva, then we would say that the methods for developing and increasing compassion, bodhichitta and so forth are the conditions that enable someone to become a bodhisattva in the first place and then to continue on the path and to achieve enlightenment. So, in terms of the Buddha having taught the path and having taught the methods for developing and increasing compassion, prajna and bodhichitta, we speak of a bodhisattva as being a son of the Buddha.

There is also another common way in which a bodhisattva is regarded as "a son of the victorious one, a son of the conqueror." The way it is explained in the commentaries is "the continuation of the lineage of the family." For instance, if someone is born as a prince, then having been trained and matured, that prince will eventually take up all of the work of his father, the king. Whatever the king has done, similarly, the prince eventually will do. From that point of view one can say that the family lineage has not been severed, that it continues. Similarly, having been taught the paths of prajna, compassion, and bodhichitta by the Buddha, if a bodhisattva trains him or herself and eventually takes up the role of the Buddha, we say that the family lineage is not severed.

Question: Could you expand on what you mean by non-dual? What that has to do with prajna?
Rinpoche: There are two different meanings to the term non-dual. One is: free from something looked at and something looking at it; the other is: freedom from conceiving existence and conceiving non-existence.

Chapter 13

BUDDHIST PILGRIMAGE SITES
by *Kai Jensen*

INTRODUCTION

For 2000 years pilgrims from all traditions of Buddhism have traveled to India and Nepal to visit places of significance in the life of Buddha Shakyamuni. After the Buddha's cremation, the ashes and relics of his body from the funeral pyre were divided into eight parts, and were placed in memorial stupas at the major sites of pilgrimage: at places such as Lumbini, where the Buddha was born; Bodhgaya, the place of his enlightenment beneath the bodhi tree; Sarnath, the site of his first teaching of the dharma; Rajgir, where the Buddha stayed most often and many of his teachings were given; and Kushinagar, the place of his paranirvana. The great Buddhist emperor of most of India, Ashoka, raised stupas and memorial columns at these places and other sites where the Buddha had visited and taught. Chinese pilgrims to India in the fifth and seventh centuries CE wrote of the splendors of the monasteries and temples clustered at the pilgrimage sites. Great universities stood near places such as Rajgir, institutions where monks received advanced training, and interpretations of the dharma were refined.

In the twelfth and thirteenth centuries, however, the sites of Buddhist pilgrimage in northern India were overrun by Moslem invaders. Monasteries and temples were burnt, and Buddhist universities such as Nalanda and Vikramashila were destroyed. The pilgrimage sites were neglected and in many cases lost to knowledge for the next 600 years under Moslem and Hindu rule, until they became an object of study for British archaeologists in the nineteenth century. The excavations uncovered inscriptions and relics that confirmed the location of the key sites.

From the early twentieth century figures such as Anagarika Dharmapala and U Chandramani worked to restore and preserve the Buddhist pilgrimage sites. Today the major sites are again surrounded by temples and monasteries, and guesthouses for the thousands of pilgrims who visit them each year. Arising from the work of the archaeologists, many sites include museums displaying the statues, carvings, and inscriptions that have been recovered.

For students of Tibetan Buddhist traditions, the range of pilgrimage sites in India and Nepal is wider, and even the sites from the life of the Buddha have additional resonance, as they are also associated with the tantric mahasiddhas whose teachings form the foundation of Tibetan Buddhism. Masters such as Atisha, Dharmakirti, Shantideva, and Padmasambhava studied and debated at the Buddhist universities of Nalanda or Vikramashila. Sites that are not part of the historical record of the Buddha's life have deep significance for the Tibetan tradition: Amravati, where the Buddha taught the Kalachakra tantra after his paranirvana, or Sankyasha, where he descended to earth after teaching his mother in the Tushita Heaven. The lake of Tso Pema was formed miraculously from the fire in which soldiers attempted to burn Padmasambhava, and it was from there that he set off to bring Buddhism to Tibet. The great stupa at Swayambunath was originally the flower of a lotus discovered by the bodhisattva Manjushri; the hill beneath it was the stalk on which the flower grew. The stupa at Boudhanath contains relics of Kashyapa, the Buddha who lived and taught before Shakyamuni. For Tibetan Buddhist students, also, India is a place where we can encounter living bodhisattvas and receive their blessings and teachings: His Holiness the Dalai Lama and His Holiness the Karmapa reside in Dharamsala.

Central to Buddhism is the objective of overcoming attachment to the things of this world through contemplation of suffering and impermanence, coupled with meditation to reveal the nature of the mind. Pilgrimage to the great Buddhist sites may seem like a form of attachment to the physical traces of the Buddha's life. On the other hand, to go on pilgrimage is to be detached for a time from the pilgrim's home and everyday concerns; it is an opportunity for sustained contemplation of the Buddha's own struggle to find a solution to suffering, and of his generosity in sharing that solution with so many students over many decades. The destruction that was visited on these sites, their loss and recent restoration, is a powerful teaching on impermanence. Pilgrims may also benefit from recognizing their own insignificance, their interchangeability with countless others who have walked among these stupas and shrines for thousands of years. Thus pilgrimage, if it is undertaken without pride, can help us to break down our egotism and develop a joyful humility, a sense of connectedness with other beings.

According to a commentary by the First Dalai Lama on the Vinaya Sutra, known as "Lung-Treng-Tik" in Tibetan, the Buddha is said to have emphasized several times the importance of pilgrimage.

> Bhikshus, after my passing away, all sons and daughters who are of good family and are faithful should, as long as they live, go to the four holy places and remember: here at Lumbini, the enlightened one was born; here at Bodhgaya he attained enlightenment, here at Sarnath he turned the wheel of dharma; and there at Kushinagar he entered Paranirvana. Bhikshus, after my passing away there will be activities such as circumambulation of these places and reverence to them. Thus it should be told to them, for they who have faith in my deeds and awareness of their own will travel to higher states. After my passing away, the new Bhikshus who come and ask of the doctrine should be told of these four places and advised that a pilgrimage to them will help purify their previously accumulated karmas or actions.

The following sections provide key points of information on the main sites of Buddhist pilgrimage in India and Nepal. For safe traveling and information on accommodation, food, routes and fares, pilgrims are recommended to consult current editions of the main travelers' guidebooks such as the *Lonely Planet* or *Rough Guides*.

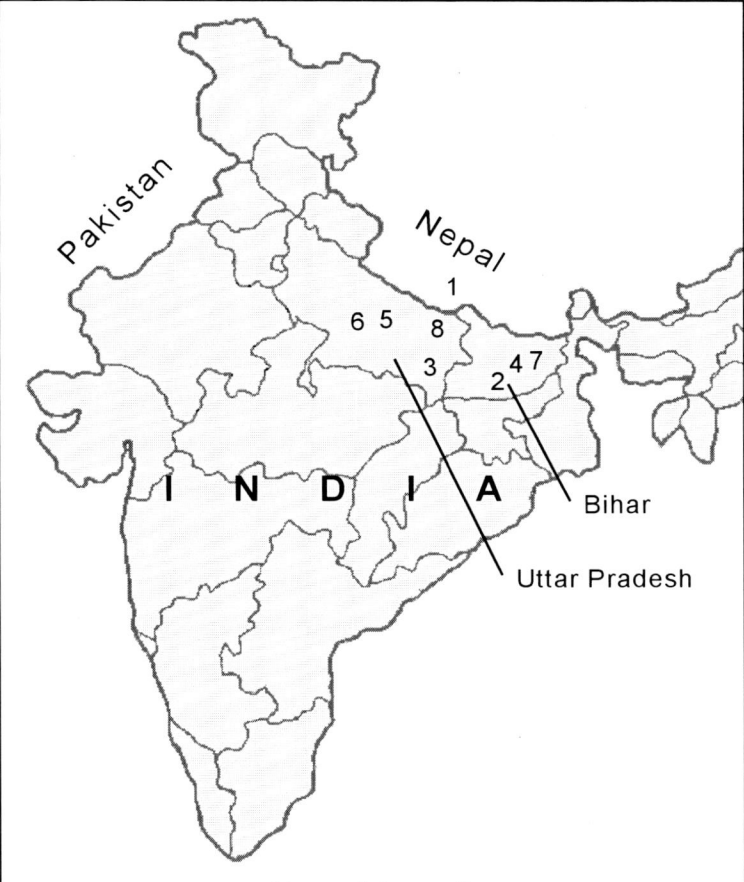

Eight Major Sites

1. **Lumbini**—birthplace of the Buddha
2. **Bodhgaya**—site of Buddha's enlightenment
3. **Sarnath**—1st turning of the Wheel of Dharma
4. **Rajgir**—2nd turning of the Wheel of Dharma, 1st Buddhist Council
5. **Shravasti**—teachings in the Jetavana Grove
6. **Sankashya**—where Lord Buddha descended from Tushita Heaven
7. **Nalanda**—site of the great monastic university
8. **Kushinagar**—where Buddha entered mahaparanirvana

LUMBINI—BIRTHPLACE OF THE BUDDHA

The birthplace of Prince Siddhartha, who became Buddha Shakyamuni, is Lumbini in Nepal. The Buddha's mother Mahamaya (Mayadevi), queen of the kingdom of Sakya, was traveling from Kapilvastu to her parents' home to give birth. She had dreamt that a white elephant pierced her side with its tusk. Stopping her journey to rest and bathe in a garden at Lumbini, the queen felt the birth coming on. Holding the branch of a sal tree for support, she gave birth to the baby who was later named Siddhartha. The baby emerged from the queen's side, took seven steps and announced that this was his last birth. At each step lotuses bloomed beneath his feet. Queen Mahamaya died a few weeks after her son was born.

The Buddhist emperor Ashoka erected four stupas and a stone pillar at Lumbini in 249 CE, and it was visited by the Chinese pilgrims Fa Hien and Huien Tsiang in approximately 399-414 CE and 635-640 CE respectively. With the destruction of

Buddhism in India the site was lost and overgrown, but the pillar that Ashoka placed there was rediscovered by archaeologists in the late nineteenth century. Today Lumbini, in the Terai region of Nepal, is a sacred precinct comprising eight square kilometers of gardens, temples, museums, and historical sites.

The site identified as the actual birthplace of Buddha is within the Sacred Garden at the southern end of Lumbini. A marker stone inside the Mayadevi Temple is said to mark the exact spot. Pilgrims enter the temple chamber to circumambulate this stone. The temple also contains a stone frieze of the birth dating from the third or fourth century CE. The Ashokan pillar stands beside the temple, and just to the south is the water tank Puskarni where Mahamaya is said to have bathed before giving birth, and where the baby Siddhartha was washed—a pool described by Huien Tsiang as "clear and bright as a mirror and the surface covered with a mixture of flowers." A number of ruined stupas and temples stand near the pool.

North of the Sacred Garden are many modern temples and shrines built by both Mahayana and Theravadan Buddhists, including an international nuns' center named after the Buddha's stepmother and first nun, Gautami. The temples and centers include Burmese, Chinese, Nepalese, Indian, Japanese, Thai and Tibetan Buddhist traditions. There is also a museum with material from the various excavations in the region on display, together with religious manuscripts and sculptures, and a research institute with an impressive library. At the northern end of Lumbini stands the forty-one meter tall Peace Stupa.

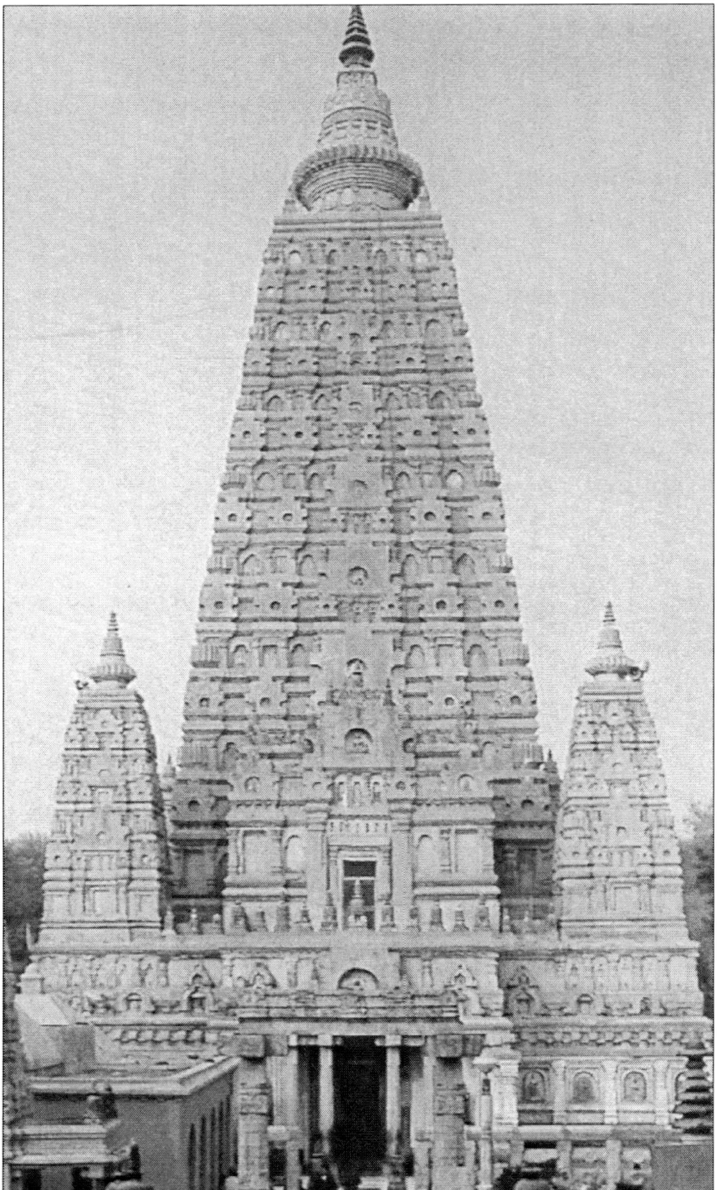

BODHGAYA—SITE OF BUDDHA'S ENLIGHTENMENT AND GAYA

The holiest of all Buddhist sites is Bodhgaya, the place where the Buddha attained supreme enlightenment more than 2,500 years ago, sitting beneath a pipal or bodhi tree, on a cushion of kusha grass. Here he resisted the assaults of the forces of Mara, the evil one, trying to prevent him from finding the path to liberation. The Buddha gently touched the fingers of his left hand to the ground, calling the earth to witness the countless births that had prepared him for this, his greatest deed, in his final incarnation. Many statues of the Buddha reproduce the bumispara (touching the earth) mudra.

The ornately carved Mahabodhi temple, with its beautiful golden Buddha statue, marks the spot where the Buddha is said to have sat; at one time a pillar erected by the emperor Ashoka stood on this spot. Sprouting beside the base of the temple is a bodhi tree that is a descendant of the original tree. The Mahabodhi temple was built some time between the visits to Bodhgaya of the two Chinese pilgrims whose detailed accounts have survived: Fa Hien in the early fifth century CE, and Huien Tsiang early in the seventh century. It has been repaired and restored repeatedly over the centuries, often through donations from pilgrims, and most recently, in the nineteenth century, by the king of Burma. The restoration was part of the work of restoring Bodhgaya from a state of neglect, led by Anagarika Dharmapala (see the entry for Sarnath) in the nineteenth and early twentieth centuries. In 1949 the Bodh Gaya Temple Act established a committee of four Buddhists and four Hindus to manage the temple and its grounds.

The temple precinct is marked off by stone railings that date from the second century BCE, and devout pilgrims over the centuries have erected a number of small stupas within and around this. The many smaller stupas to the north contain relics such as hair and nails of arhats. It is believed that if we throw our hair and nails there we will be born in the higher realms.

The Buddha is said to have remained near the bodhi tree for another seven weeks after he attained enlightenment. A marble walkway marks the place where the Buddha performed walking meditation for seven days afterwards, and a stupa, the spot where he sat for a week, gazing at the tree in gratitude.

Towards the right of the stupa is a Tara shrine containing a small image of Tara, which is said to have spoken to Lord Atisha at Bodhgaya.

Entry to the gardens surrounding the central precinct is free, but visitors pay a small charge to leave their shoes at the gate. Outside the entrance to the gardens is a lively and colorful strip of eating places and shops selling pilgrim memorabilia. The whole area is continuously busy during the day with groups of pilgrims, Hindu as well as Buddhist. Hindus regard the Buddha as an incarnation of Vishnu, and often visit Bodhgaya as part of a pilgrimage to the Hindu pilgrimage site at Gaya, fifteen kilometers to the north. Gaya is one of the seven holy cities of India. The Buddha visited it, and it was there that he taught the Fire Sermon to which the poet T. S. Eliot refers in *The Waste Land*.

As with the other major Buddhist pilgrimage sites, Bodhgaya contains many temples and guesthouses erected by the various traditions of Buddhism. Pilgrims can obtain good quality accommodation here at moderate rates. His Holiness the Dalai Lama has a number of times delivered the Kalachakra initiation at a large open area near the sacred gardens.

SARNATH—FIRST TURNING OF THE WHEEL OF DHARMA

Some weeks after he attained enlightenment, the Buddha first gave teachings—turned the wheel of the dharma—in the deer park at Sarnath, near modern-day Varanasi. This is why a symbol of the dharma in many Buddhist traditions is the dharmachakra, a wheel flanked by two listening deer. The Buddha gave his first discourse, on the Four Noble Truths, to the five followers who had abandoned him when he renounced asceticism to follow the path of moderation, the Middle-way. Sarnath is also the place where the Buddha first ordained monks, and where he first held a meditation retreat through the monsoon season. The Buddhist emperor Ashoka built a temple and meditated here, and set up one of his carved columns. The capital of the ruined column—

four lions roaring the news of the dharma in the cardinal directions—has become the state symbol of modern India, and is kept in the archaeological museum at Sarnath.

The oldest surviving structure at Sarnath is the weathered Dharmek Stupa, made of huge bricks with residual carvings. It was first built in the second century BCE, and its current form dates from the fifth century CE. The stupa marks the place where the Buddha gave his second discourse, on non-self. The Dhammarajika Stupa, marking the site of the first discourse, was dismantled in 1794 on the orders of the local rajah: its materials were used to construct a market in nearby Varanasi. Between these stupas lie foundations and columns of monasteries that were razed by the Muslim invaders who drove Buddhism from India in the twelfth and thirteenth centuries CE. Only a mound remains of the stupa that is said to mark the spot where the Buddha approached his former followers, and where, although they had intended to ignore his approach, they spontaneously rose to their feet in respect because of his radiant appearance.

These ruins stand in a peaceful park; along the nearby roads are temples built by a number of Buddhist traditions. Sarnath as a peaceful precinct for Buddhist pilgrims was largely made possible by the activities of the Mahabodhi Society in the early twentieth century. This society was founded by Anagarika Dharmapala, who made it his life's work to restore and cherish the Buddhist holy places of India. A few hundred meters east of the Dharmek Stupa stands the Mulagandhakuti Vihara, the temple completed by the Society in 1931. Anagarika Dharmapala was cremated nearby, and his ashes are housed in a small stupa behind the main shrine of the temple; the shrine itself contains relics believed to be those of the Buddha. A bodhi tree nearby is another descendant of the original tree at Bodhgaya.

Rajgir—Vulture Peak Mountain, Second Turning of the Wheel of Dharma & First Buddhist Council

Of all the sites for Buddhist pilgrimage, Rajgir is perhaps most evocative of the Buddha's work after his enlightenment, as a teacher and leader of a growing monastic movement. Walking among the hills and ruins of Rajgir the pilgrim can visit many places where events of the Buddha's life occurred, and where he gave important teachings.

Rajgir was the capital of the Magadha Kingdom, and the largest city in the central Ganges valley in the Buddha's day. While he was still a wandering ascetic, Siddhartha met Bimbisara, king of Magadha, and declined his invitation to join his court, but promised, once he discovered the path to liberation, to return and teach it to the king and his subjects. After he attained enlightenment at Bodhgaya and began teaching at Sarnath and Gaya, the Buddha returned to Rajgir, accompanied by 1000 monks, to fulfill this promise.

King Bimbisara gave the Buddha and his monks a warm welcome, and the king and many of his senior courtiers became devoted followers and patrons of the dharma. The king donated a park, the Veluvana or Bamboo Grove, to the Buddha as the site for a monastery. Long afterwards, the mahasiddha Asanga, who received teachings directly from the Lord Maitreya, is said to have built a small temple in the Veluvana and lived here for several years.

With such support from King Bimbisara and his court, the Buddha spent much time in Rajgir: in particular he stayed here for the second, third and fourth rainy season retreats after his enlightenment, delivering many of his best-known discourses in the Veluvana and Jivakambavana (see below). His disciples Shariputra and Moggallana were citizens of Rajgir who joined the growing monastic community.

The king's personal physician, Jivaka, would treat the Buddha when he became ill. Jivaka donated a mango grove to him, just outside the city walls, building huts and pavilions there for the accommodation of the Buddha and his monks. This complex, the Jivakambavana, was excavated by archaeologists in the mid-twentieth century CE, and visitors can trace the layout of a typical monastery of the Buddha's time.

A winding path leads from the Jivakambavana to a small hill, the Gijjhakuta or Vulture's Peak Mountain, which was a favorite place of the Buddha's for solitary meditation. He also delivered some of his most important teachings here, including teachings on the Prajnaparamita—the perfection of wisdom—and the Lotus Sutra, which makes clear that Buddha nature is inherent in all beings—that we will all eventually attain enlightenment. This is also the place where Avalokiteshvara, through the blessing of the Buddha, spoke the Heart Sutra. A cave on Gijjhakuta called the Sukarakhata or the Boar's Grotto is said to be the place where Shariputra attained liberation.

King Bimbisara had a road constructed to make it easier for him to visit the Buddha on the heights of Gijjhakuta, and this still remains: two stupas are said to mark the place where the king would dismount from his chariot to continue on foot, and the place where he would require his attendants to wait while he went on to meet the Buddha alone.

As well as these many positive events, Rajgir also reminds us of the obstacles and resistance encountered by the Buddha and his followers. Some of the Buddha's own disciples, including his cousin Devadatta, split away from the Buddha's sangha and even attempted to kill him, by rolling a huge stone down on him from the heights of Gijjhakuta, and by setting a fierce elephant, Nalagiri, loose where the Buddha was known to be walking. Only the Buddha's foot was injured by the stone, and the Buddha tamed the elephant by his powers and calm presence.

King Bimbisara also encountered ill fortune: he was imprisoned and starved to death by his own son, Ajasattu, who wished to become king. A heap of stones within the old city walls is said to be Bimbisara's jail, where the old king was solaced in his slow death by looking up to the peak of Gijjhakuta, knowing that the Buddha was meditating there. Ajasattu later repented his cruel treatment of his father, and became a firm supporter of the dharma. After the Buddha's paranirvana, one eighth of his relics were given to the king of Magadha, who built a stupa over them. The site of the stupa, which long ago fell into ruins, is still marked by large stones and pillars, outside the walls of 'new' Rajgir, the later of the two abandoned cities on the site. The Buddhist emperor Ashoka also built a stupa nearby.

One other event of great importance in the history of Buddhism occurred at Rajgir. The first Buddhist Council was held here, within a few months after the Buddha's paranirvana, in the cave known as Sattapanni. This can still be visited, on the slopes of Vaibhara's Hill, to the east of old Rajgir. King Ajasattu is recorded as having erected a splendid meeting hall for the council, which was attended by 500 arhats. The Buddha's faithful follower Ananda attained liberation just in time to be allowed to participate in the council, which was led by the senior monk Mahakashyapa. Ananda, who had a superb memory about the exact wording of the Buddha's teachings expounded the Sutras, Upali, an expert on monastic discipline, expounded the Vinaya, the Buddha's rules for the community of monks, and Mahakashyapa expounded the Abhidharma. In this way the council clarified the complete canon and chanted them together to fix them in the monks' memories. These works have come down to us today as a central collection of the dharma, supplemented by the commentaries of the great masters of later days.

When the sixth Dalai Lama visited Gijjhakuta, what he saw was the cliff piled high with Sanskrit scriptures. This highlights the difference in appearances of great realized masters and ourselves. What we perceive is due to our own individual karma, something we need to understand and be mindful of when we visit sacred sites and see only ruins and empty temples.

Shravasti—Teachings in the Jetavana Grove
(rainy season retreat)

Shravasti (formerly Savatthi, the wealthy capital of ancient Kosala) is renowned as the retreat of the Buddha during twenty-four rainy seasons. The merchant Sudatta met the Buddha in Rajgir and, overjoyed with his presence, invited him to spend the next rainy season at Shravasti. Buddha asked for a peaceful place with facilities suitable for his monks. Sudatta decided to purchase a park belonging to Prince Jeta, whose original price was that the park be covered with gold pieces. Sudatta, now known as Anathapindika (incomparable alms giver) began to lay out the gold, and Jeta relented, helping to build a huge monastic complex, described in the Vinaya, which was given the name Jetavana Anathapindikarama.

Today pilgrims coming to this beautiful grove pray in the remains of the two favorite dwelling places of the Buddha. The larger of these, Gandhakuti, the Fragrant Hut, recalls the offerings of sandalwood and flowers made to the Buddha. It was probably originally a wooden building, described in the *Sumangalavilasini* as having a small internal room, a bathroom, a terrace outside where the Buddha would walk in the evening, and a 'jeweled staircase' leading up to it where talks were given to the monks. Today's ruins (dating from the fourth to seventh centuries CE) comprise a brick pavilion, terrace, stairs and a shrine. Further to the south is the smaller Kosambakuti, Buddha's other dwelling for sleeping, meditating, and talking to visitors. Like the Gandhakuti, today the Kosambakuti consists of brick ruins and encloses a shrine. Still further to the south, closer to the monastery itself, is a bodhi tree which some say comes from a seed of the original bodhi tree, others from a cutting of the daughter bodhi tree in Sri Lanka. Here pilgrims would leave their offerings in homage to the Buddha when he was away from Shravasti.

Closer to the main road are monastic ruins probably dating from the twelfth century and built over an earlier sixth century construction. There are twenty-one cells for monks, one containing a brick bed with a raised pillow. A number of statues and household implements were found here in the course of excavations. Also in the Jetavana Grove are stupas, said to commemorate revered monks across the centuries and important events in the Buddha's life, and other monastic ruins. Because the Buddha stayed at Shravasti for so much of his time, most of his discourses, including the Metta Sutta, were given in the region, and many of these talks would have occurred in these monasteries. Thus it is a fitting place to read the words of the Buddha and perhaps imagine them being spoken for the first time.

Several famous stories from the Buddha's life originated at Shravasti. It was here that the murderer Angulimala, wearing his necklace of severed fingers, met Shakyamuni and repented of his wrongdoing. His decision to become a monk and his eventual enlightenment are said to have been marked by the stupa Pakki Kuti, a little to the north of the park.

The Buddha banned his followers from performing miracles. When the Buddha himself, however, was challenged to a competition by a group of non-believers, he agreed and performed miracles, reported in the *Divyavadana*. The king of Kosala had built a hall with thrones for the competition, in the process cutting down the surrounding mango grove. As the Buddha approached, he was offered a mango by a gardener: after he ate it, the seed was planted and a fully grown and fruiting mango tree sprang up. Some versions also report the Buddha flying into the hall. On the next day, the Buddha performed a miracle by rising into the air, standing on a rainbow bridge (or maybe a thousand-petaled lotus) spanning from one horizon to the other; from his shoulder came flames and from his feet streams of water. In the second miracle, known as *mahapratiharya*, the Buddha divided himself into multiple bodies so that everyone present had his or her own Buddha to talk with. Not surprisingly the Buddha won the competition, confounding the skeptics.

Over the centuries the fortunes of Shravasti waxed and waned but it remained an important center of Buddhism. The emperor Ashoka is said to have built pillars twenty-one meters high in the grove. When the Chinese monk Fa Hien visited in the early fifth century CE, he described a luxuriant grove, with a pool and a monastery. By his account the original Jetavana temple was seven stories high and hung with rich silks with continually replenished offerings of flowers and lamps. There was also a famous sandalwood statue of the Buddha. One day a rat ran away with a burning wick in its mouth and set fire to the building, and everyone was saddened to think that the statue had been burnt. However, some days later, a small temple door was opened and the statue seen unscathed in this new position. So the monastery was rebuilt, this time two stories high, and the statue was moved back to its original place in the temple.

By the time the pilgrim Huien Tsang arrived in the 630s CE, he found only ruins. These were restored soon after, and the monastery flourished until the twelfth century. The site was identified by the English archaeologist Cunningham in 1863, and since then archaeological excavations have unearthed a number of buildings.

More recently Buddhist temples and monasteries have been built at Shravasti by Sri Lankans, Japanese, Thai and Chinese, and a stupa by Tibetan monks. There is also a Jain temple, as Shravasti is venerated as the birthplace of two Jain Tirthikas. The shrine in the Sri Lankan temple contains excellent contemporary Buddhist paintings, representing scenes from the life of the Buddha and events in Buddhist history.

Shravasti is accessible by train from Lucknow (which has an airport); the nearest station is Balrampur, seventeen kilometers away, from which pilgrims can proceed to Shravasti by bus or taxi. Many statues and objects from the Jetavana excavations are now housed in the museum in Lucknow. Some of the temples at Shravasti offer accommodation to pilgrims.

Sankashya—Where Lord Buddha Descended from Tushita Heaven

Both the great Chinese Buddhist pilgrims, Fa Hien in the fifth century CE, and Huien Tsiang in the seventh century, found substantial monastic communities at Sankashya. They identified this as the place where the Buddha had descended from the Tushita Heaven after spending a rainy season retreat there, teaching the Abhidharma to his mother, Queen Mayadevi, who had died shortly after his birth and had been born in Tushita as a male god. The emperor Ashoka erected one of his pillars here, topped with an elephant capital.

The British archaeologist General Cunningham identified Sankashya as a place near a village west of Farruhabad, above Kanpur, on the Ganges. It remains a relatively neglected site.

NALANDA—SITE OF THE GREAT MONASTIC UNIVERSITY

The great Buddhist university of Nalanda Mahavihara was built beside the stupa containing the ashes of Shariputra, one of the Buddha's most devoted followers. Only eleven kilometers from Rajgir, the village of Nalanda is said to have been Shariputra's birthplace, and the Buddha often stayed, meditated and taught in a mango grove there. The monastic university of Nalanda, however, did not arise on this site until almost 1000 years later.

The university did not yet exist when the Chinese pilgrim monk Fa Hien passed this way in the early fifth century CE: he noted only the stupa of Shariputra and a temple erected there by the Buddhist Emperor Ashoka; there is no mention of a center of learning. Two centuries later, however, when Huien Tsiang, another traveling Chinese monk, came to Nalanda, he found a great university with libraries, colleges, towers and temples, famous throughout Asia for the learning of its graduates.

Thus the university of Nalanda appears to have been founded by the Gupta emperors of northern India in the fifth century. It grew and flourished until in the ninth century it is said to have housed 8500 monks and 1500 teachers. Nalanda played an important role in the spread of Buddhism to Tibet. Three teachers who taught Buddhism to the Tibetans had studied at Nalanda: Kamalasila, Shantarakshita and, above all, Padmasambhava. Many of the great Indian Buddhist masters—Dignaga, Dharmakirti, Dharmapala and Shantideva—also studied or taught here.

In the Tibetan Buddhist tradition the six ornaments (great masters at Nalanda between the second and tenth centuries CE) were Nagarjuna, Asanga, Gunaprabha, Aryadeva, Vasubhandu, and Sakyaprabha. If we add Dignaga and Dharmakirti they become the eight ornaments. (It should be noted that in the historical record Nalanda was not founded until some centuries after the lifetimes of Nagarjuna and Aryadeva.)

Nalanda appears to have been an institution for advanced scholars: students were only admitted if they satisfied a rigorous test of their knowledge of Buddhist texts and philosophy, administered by the scholar who kept the gate. Debate on the Buddhist texts and their concepts was the main activity of the institution, supplemented by secular topics such as logic, grammar, astronomy and medicine; there were lay students as well as monks. The university had not one but three libraries. Sanskrit was the language of instruction of Nalanda, but many other languages were spoken there, as the students came from all the Asian countries.

Nalanda was the foremost of several great Buddhist universities of the time; there were others at nearby Odantapuri, and at Vikramashila. Nalanda was funded partly by lay students' fees, partly by the revenue of feudal villages donated by the emperors for its support, and partly by other donations. The university's learning was famous throughout Asia, and its degrees were seen as a qualification for a range of careers in the royal courts. Indeed, Nalanda's reputation was so high that people sometimes forged copies of its degrees for their own advancement.

As with many other holy Buddhist sites in northern India, Nalanda was destroyed by the Moslem invaders early in the thirteenth century CE. The Tibetan monk Dharmaswamin was a student at Nalanda when it was first raided, and helped the aged abbot of the university into hiding nearby. They returned for a while, but had to flee the area in the face of further raids.

On any given day at Nalanda 100 classes would be delivered, and in the afternoon and evening devotional services would be held in each college. There would be annual holidays when the monks would visit the pilgrimage sites such as Rajgir, and Bodhgaya, 80 kilometers to the south-west. For a modern pilgrim it is enriching to think of the monks who lived in the now ruined colleges, visiting the same pilgrimage places as oneself.

Like many other Buddhist sites, Nalanda was excavated by British archaeologists in the 1860s; it was definitively identified when the official seal of the university was discovered. Today, for a modest entrance fee, pilgrims can wander through the ruined colleges and temples, and circumambulate the huge ruined stupa of Shariputra. The site is easily reached by bus or taxi from Patna or Gaya, or from the nearest railway station, at Bhaktiyarpur.

Most Westerners are conscious only of the European university tradition that started in medieval Bologna. Nalanda is a monument to the older intellectual tradition of Buddhism, with its searching analysis of the nature of human consciousness.

KUSHINAGAR—WHERE BUDDHA ENTERED
MAHAPARANIRVANA

At Kushinagar, in his eighty-first year, the Buddha lay down and waited for the passing that he had predicted was approaching. At the nearby town of Pava, the Buddha had accepted an offering of food from the metalsmith Cunda, containing meat which had gone bad. Afterwards, as he lay, the Buddha sent his follower Ananda to reassure Cunda that, far from being a negative thing, offering the Buddha his last meal was a highly auspicious act.

At Kushinagar the Buddha lay in the lion posture (on his right side, resting his head on his hand), between two tall sala trees. Prior to his passing Buddha gave teachings to a wandering ascetic named Subhadda, and ordained him as a monk. As a result of this Subhadda subsequently attained liberation. In his last moments the Buddha said his final words to his followers: "Now monks, I say to you, all conditioned things are subject to decay —strive on with diligence."

Kushinagar is smaller and more peaceful than the better-known pilgrimage sites of Bodhgaya and Sarnath. Archaeologists have found the remains of ten monasteries here, dating from the fourth to the eleventh centuries CE. The place is believed to have been a thriving pilgrimage site in the third through fifth centuries CE, and emperor Ashoka built a column and a great stupa here. By the time the Chinese pilgrim Huien Tsiang visited it in the seventh century, however, it was all but deserted. He saw a shrine containing a magnificent large statue of the reclining Buddha.

The decline of Kushinagar continued, and archaeologists believe it ceased to be a site of pilgrimage even before the Islamic invasion of the twelfth century. The name itself was lost, and British archaeologists in the nineteenth century had a lengthy scholarly debate before the village Kasia was confirmed to be Kushinagar at the end of the century. The Buddha Mahaparanirvana shrine was unearthed from between a huge mound of bricks surrounded by thorn trees. The reclining Buddha statue had been broken in fragments, and had to be pieced back together.

In the 1900s a Burmese monk, Venerable U Chandramani, visited Kushinagar as a pilgrim and decided to stay there. He built a temple and guesthouse where he began to host other pilgrims. The Burmese center is the oldest of the monasteries; Japanese, Korean, Thai and Tibetan temples have since been built. In 1956, to commemorate the 2500th year of the Buddhist Era, the Indian Government erected the new Buddha Mahaparanirvana Temple. The reclining Buddha statue is today covered in a layer of gold leaf pressed on it by the hands of pilgrims.

The large stupa immediately behind the temple contains, at its center, pieces of charcoal and blackened earth, thought to be from the Buddha's cremation pyre. A kilometer to the south, the ruined Rhambar Stupa, a weathered mound of bricks fifteen meters high, marks the spot where the Buddha's body is said to have been cremated.

This is also the place where an enormous statue of Maitreya, the future Buddha—some 150 meters high—is to be constructed.

To reach Kushinagar, visitors should go by train to Gorakhpur, and then catch a bus or tempo for the remaining 51 kilometers (asking to be let out at the Buddha Dwar gate). There are several moderately expensive hotels at Kushinagar, or pilgrims can make donation to stay in the Myanmar Buddhist Temple and Guesthouse.

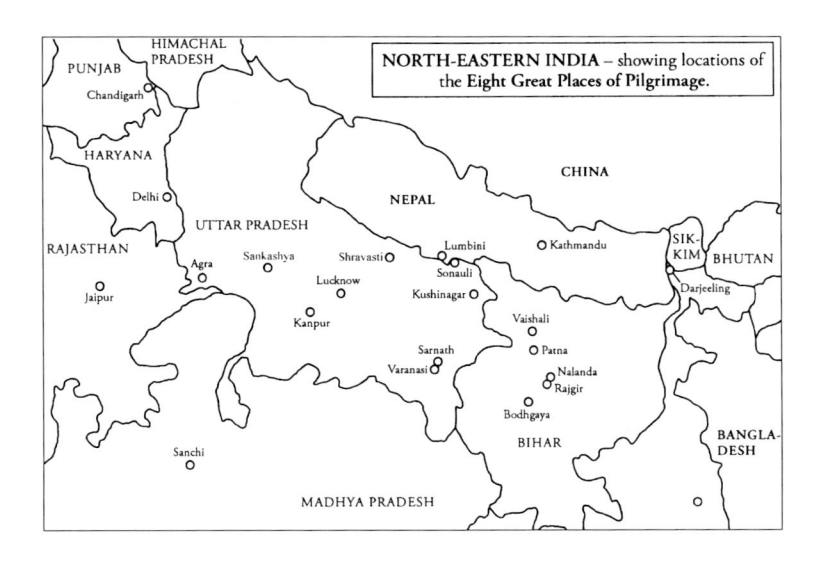

180   *The History of Buddhism in India*

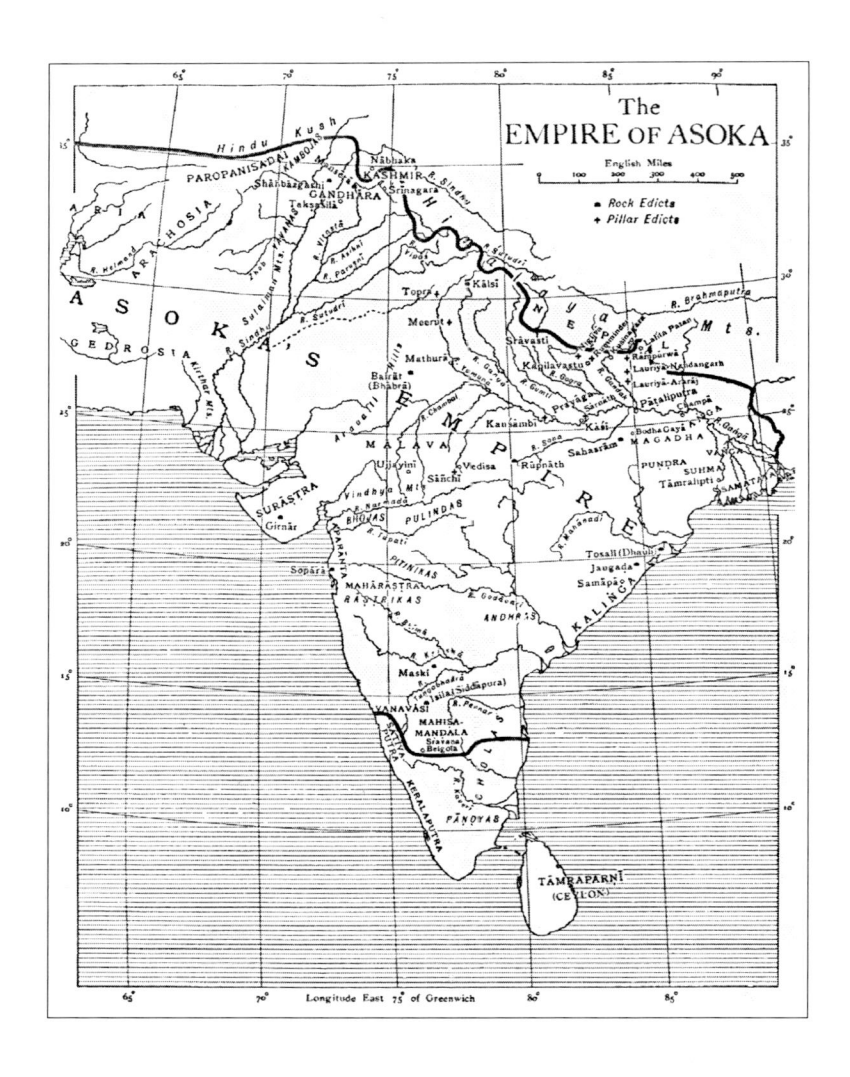

A Map of India in the time of the Buddhist King Ashoka

Buddhist Pilgrimage Sites   181

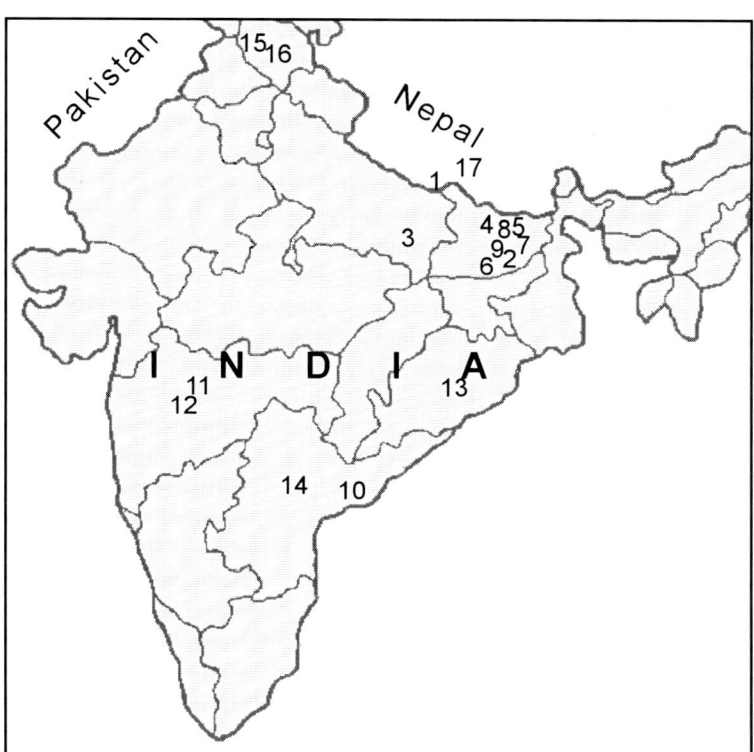

ADDITIONAL SITES
1. **Kapilvastu / Kapliavatthu**—home of Buddha's family
2. **Nairanjana & Pragbodhi**—where Buddha practiced austerities
3. **Kaushambi / Kosambhi** 4. **Kesariya**
5. **Hajipur**—where Ananda's ashes were enshrined
6. **Gurpa**—where Mahakashyapa waits for Maitreya
7. **Vikramasila**—great Buddhist University
8. **Vaishali / Vesali**—2nd Buddhist Council
9. **Patna**—3rd Buddhist Council
10. **Amravati**—where Buddha taught Kalachakra
11. **Ajanta Caves** 12. **Ellora Caves**
13. **Dhauli Hill** 14. **Nagarjuna Konda**
15. **Tso Pema** 16. **Dharamsala**
17. **Boudhanath Stupa / Swayambunath Stupa**

Kapilvastu—Home of Buddha's Family

Kapilvastu was the capital of the Sakya kingdom, where the young Prince Siddhartha grew up, married, and became the father of a son. In the palace at Kapilvastu his father, King Shuddhodana, tried to shelter Siddhartha from life's harsh realities, fearing a prediction that the prince would give up his position as prince and heir to the throne, to become a spiritual leader. Despite the king's care, however, the prince encountered an old man, a sick man and a corpse, and inferred the extent of life's suffering. To search for a way by which all people might escape from this suffering, he left his father's palace, his wife and child, and took up the life of a wandering ascetic. After his enlightenment he returned to Kapilvastu to visit his family and give teachings; and his stepmother, Gautami, and son, Rahula, became members of the Buddhist sangha.

Both India and Nepal have claimed to contain the site of the historical Kapilvastu. It appears more likely that the Indian site, near Piprahwa, about thirteen kilometers from Lumbini, is the correct one. In 1898 a soapstone casket was unearthed in a stupa there, with an inscription that is the earliest decipherable writing ever found in India. The most likely translation is that the burnt bones contained in the casket are relics of the Buddha, placed there by his Sakya relations. Further excavations in the 1970s unearthed seals with the name Kapilvastu, a strong confirmation of the site's historical identity. Claims for the Nepalese site, Tilaurakot, are less specific: they are based on evidence that it was a fortified settlement dating back to the Buddha's period, and that it is near Lumbini.

The main stupa at Kapilvastu was first built in the fifth century BCE, then built over with a second stupa about 150 years later; a third and larger stupa was built later, and this is the one visible today. The oldest of the stupas contained caskets that held fragments of charred human bones, very likely relics of the Buddha. The ruins of a large monastery stand a little to the east of the stupa, and here a seal was found with the words "Kapilavatthu Bhikshu Sangha." The remains of two other monasteries and a public hall are nearby. The actual town of Kapilavatthu stood about a kilometer south of the stupa and monasteries.

LAURIYA NANDANGARH—
WHERE BUDDHA WAS SELF-ORDAINED AS A MONK

Lauriya Nandangarh is situated in the state of Bihar. It lies at a distance of approximately 22 km from the district of Bettiah. Lauriya Nandangarh boasts of housing the Ashokan pillar, comprising of the six Ashokan Edicts. As per the version of the historians as well as the archaeologists, as many as forty pillars were built here by Emperor Ashoka. However, today only one pillar exists in complete form, at its initial location in Lauriya Nandangarh. The height of the pillar is more than twelve meters.

One of the major attractions of Lauriya Nandangarh is a large stupa (*Namdak-drong chorten*), considered to be the one of the biggest stupas in India. The massive stupa is 24m in height and has a circumference of almost 457m.[33]

NAIRANJANA & PRAGBODHI— WHERE BUDDHA PRACTICED AUSTERITIES

The Nairanjana river, close to Bodhgaya, is where the Buddha engaged in ascetic practices.

The mountain Pragbodhi near Bodhgaya is said to be the last of the places where the Prince Siddhartha practiced as an ascetic for six years until shortly before he attained enlightenment. The mountain, today called Dhungeswara, can be reached on foot from Bodhgaya, or by taking the bus along the old Gaya road, alighting at the village Kiriyama and walking from there. According to tradition, Prince Siddhartha stayed in a small cave halfway up the mountain.

Towards the north-east is where the Brahmin girl Sajata offered the Buddha milk.

KAUSHAMBHI

The Buddha visited Kaushambhi, in Uttar Pradesh, twice, in the sixth and ninth years after his enlightenment, and gave several teachings here, such as the Kosambiya Sutra. At that time the city was a major center of trade and communications in northern India. The emperor Ashoka erected a pillar here to commemorate the Buddha's presence. Sculptures and other antiquities discovered at Kaushambhi are now in the collection of the museum at nearby Allahabad.

Kesariya

A massive stupa was raised at Kesariya (formerly Kessaputta) to commemorate an incident near the end of the Buddha's life, when he gave his begging bowl to persuade a group of people to stop following him and return to their homes. The Chinese pilgrims Fa Hien and Huien Tsiang visited this stupa, which can still be seen today, with its five terraces of different shapes. Kesariya can be reached by turning off the Musaffarpur-Motihari road at Pipra.

Hajipur—Where Ananada's Ashes were Enshrined

Hajipur is a small village situated in the state of Bihar, about 10 km from the capital city of Patna. In ancient times it was known as Ukkacala and was the first village one came to after crossing the River Ganges at Patna. Hajipur is known as the venue of the Cula Goplalaka Sutra, a Middle Length Discourse taught by the Buddha and also for housing some of the ashes of Ananda, the close disciple and personnel attendant of the Buddha.

It is believed that Ananda, after realizing that his life was drawing to an end, headed north from Rajgir. Hearing this, King Ajasattu, escorted by his entire staff, went after Ananda with the intention of requesting him to stay. Meanwhile the people of Vaishali, upon hearing the news, started gathering at the banks of the River Ganges to welcome him. When King Ajasattu caught up with Ananda, he was already in the middle of the river.

The people of Vaishali on one bank and King Ajasattu and his entourage on the other, each requested Ananda to come over to their side. In order to avoid disappointment and possible conflict, Ananda rose into the air and disappeared into a ball of flames with his ashes falling on both banks of the river. On either bank a stupa was built at the same spot where the ashes fell. With the river changing its course over time, the stupa on the southern bank got washed away. The one on the northern bank is now a grassy mound which a Hindu temple known as Ramchaura Mandir built over it.

Gurpa—Where Mahakashyapa Waits for Maitreya

The mountain Gurpa stands some thirty-three kilometers from Gaya (near Bodhgaya), beyond Fatipur on the Fatipur road. From the village of Gurpa, paths lead up to the mountain beyond the railway line. This is said to be the place where Mahakashyapa, who led the monastic communities after the Buddha's paranirvana, went at the end of his own life. He is said to have opened and entered a cavity in the rocks where he remains to this day, deep in meditation. It is said that when the future Buddha, Maitreya, appears in the world, he will go to Gurpa and awaken Mahakashyapa so he can receive the Buddha's robe from him. It is also said that Asanga spent many years meditating here before he received teachings directly from Maitreya.

Vikramashila—The Great Buddhist University

The ruins of the Buddhist university of Vikramashila has been partially excavated at the village of Antichak in the Bhagalpur district of Bihar. The university was reputedly established by King Dharmapala (783-820 CE), and the mahasiddhas Atisha and Naropa are said to have been gate-keeper scholars there. The ruins comprise the pillars of a gatehouse and a quadrangle with a temple in the center, surrounded by buildings that contained monks' cells.

Vaishali—Second Buddhist Council

The Buddha made many long visits to Vaishali and gave numerous teachings there. It was the place where he gave his last discourse before his paranirvana. A century after the Buddha's passing, the second Buddhist council took place at Vaishali.

Following the Buddha's enlightenment and first turning of the wheel of dharma at Sarnath, he stayed for a prolonged period at Rajgir, the capital of King Bimbisara, where he first ordained monks. From Rajgir, he then went to Vaishali, the capital of the Licchavis, on the north bank of the Ganges not far from the modern Patna. This is the place where the Buddha was eventually persuaded to ordain nuns.

The city is said to have had three lines of walls with gates with towers, and to have been very prosperous and grand. It is said that King Bimbisara had the road from Rajgir to the Ganges improved to make it easier for the Buddha to visit. The Buddha stayed at Vaishali several more times.

It was in Vaishali that the Buddha eventually experienced the sickness that led to his passing, and gave his last public teaching. From here he set out for Kushinagar, where his paranirvana took place. It is said that the Licchavis persisted in following him on his last departure from the city, and did not return home until the Buddha had given them his alms bowl, and frightened them with the illusion of a flooded river.

A temple was built in Vaishali to house the Buddha's alms bowl, but the bowl was later taken away to Peshawar by King Kanishka after he conquered Vaishali in the second century CE. Over the next 800 years Chinese pilgrims visiting northern India reported seeing the bowl there. The Islamic invasion of northern India resulted in the destruction of the temple where the bowl was kept in Peshawar, but the bowl itself survives and today is housed in a small Muslim shrine at Kandhara in Afghanistan.

Some of the best known events of the Buddha's life took place in Vaishali. The Buddha's foster mother, Mahaprajapati Gautami, made a pilgrimage to Vaishali from Kapilvastu with 500 other women of the Buddha's own people, the Sakyas. The Buddha three times refused their requests to be ordained, but they persisted, shaving their heads and putting on orange monastic robes, until eventually he agreed to ordain them as nuns.

It was in Vaishali, too, that the Buddha during his first visit stayed in a mango grove belonging to the famous and wealthy courtesan Ambapali. She was inspired by his teachings, and invited the Buddha and his retinue to visit her home the next day to share a meal with her. The Licchavi nobles also wanted to entertain the Buddha the next day, but Ambapali said she would not give up the honor of hosting him for 100,000 gold coins. After the meal she gave the Buddha her mango grove, which became the site of a famous monastery. Ambapali later became a nun and composed a poem about the loss of her beauty in ageing—one of the earliest Indian poems by a woman to survive.

Because Vaishali was an important center of the Buddha's activities, after his cremation an eighth portion of his relics were entrusted to the Licchavis, who raised a stupa to house them. The remains of this stupa can still be seen near the large rectangular tank (or pond) called Kharauna Pokhar, believed to have been used in the coronation of rulers of the Vajjian Confederacy, of which the Licchavis were a leading tribe.

About 110 years after the Buddha's paranirvana and the First Buddhist Council at Rajgir, in the year 376 BCE, the Second Buddhist Council is said to have been held at Vaishali. Accounts of the background of the council vary, but it appears to have been convened to debate proposals by monks in Vaishali that ten precepts for monks should be relaxed or introduced: among others, that monks should be permitted to store away salt, to eat after the noon hour, to use bedding, mats and robes that departed from the prescribed size, to drink beverages that had been forbidden, and to accept gifts of gold and silver. The last proposal was the most controversial.

A group of elder monks, meeting in a garden in Vaishali, branded these requests the "Ten Unlawful Things" and condemned them. They convened a gathering of 700 monks for a group recitation of the sutras and rules of discipline.

In response to this rejection, however, the Vaishali monks then held a council of their own, of 10,000 monks, who referred to themselves as the Mahasanghika or "Members of the Great Order." This appears to have resulted in divisions in Buddhism between this group and the Theravadan or "Teaching of the

Elders." Over the next 100 years further sects arose within these two broad divisions. Some scholars argue that this prefigured the division of Buddhism into Hinayana (Theravadan) and Mahayana—between an emphasis on monastic withdrawal, and an emphasis on compassionate engagement.

After the main stupa at Vaishali was rediscovered in 1958, archaeologists' excavations confirmed that it is very ancient. Originally made of rammed earth, it was repeatedly enlarged with layers of brick over the next few hundred years. King Ashoka is said to have opened the stupa and to have removed nine tenths of the Buddha's relics from it, so these could be placed in the stupas he was building in other parts of his empire. He restored a small portion of the relics to the Licchavis' stupa, however, and they remained there until archaeologists removed them: they are now stored in the Patna Museum.

A little way north of the Licchavis' stupa are the remains of another large stupa, constructed by King Ashoka, and next to it a statue of a lion on a tall pillar, similar to the columns raised by King Ashoka at many pilgrimage sites, but in a different style. It is thought to have provided the model for the Ashokan columns.

Because the site of Vaishali has often been flooded by the nearby Gandak River, little of the remains of the once great city survive. A small archaeological museum contains some of the sculptures and artifacts that have been recovered.

Patna

The city of Patna, capital of Bihar, was visited several times by the Buddha; he passed through it on his final journey to Kushinagar. There is an excellent collection of Buddhist art in the Patna Museum on Buddha Marg. The remains of a Mauryian period palace at Kumrahar are said to have been the palace of the great Buddhist emperor Ashoka.

Amravati—Where Buddha Taught Kalachakra

Amravati is considered the most sacred site of Buddhist pilgrimage in South India. To students of the Vajrayana, it is revered as the place where the Buddha, shortly after his paranirvana, first delivered the Kalachakra root tantra, at the request of the king of Shambhala, King Suchandra (Dawa Sangpo).

Amravati is also of importance to other Buddhist traditions, however, as a place where a great stupa was erected over relics of the Buddha, reputedly by the Buddhist emperor Ashoka. There was a large Buddhist monastic community here well before the start of the Christian era, and some foundations of the monasteries can still be seen.

Of the stupa, only the foundation mound has survived, although archaeologists have gained a good idea of the former structure from its fragmentary remains. The stupa was the largest in South India, with a dome made of pale green limestone that stood about eighteen meters high; the stupa as a whole would have been about thirty meters high. The upper part of the dome was probably decorated with plaster garlands. A beautifully carved railing surrounded the base of the stupa, with four gateways, one in each of the cardinal directions. One of the gateways has been reconstructed, and visitors can admire its carvings of scenes from the Buddha's heroic life. The gateways were guarded by sculptures of lions.

The small archaeological museum contains some fine carvings from Amravati's long history of Buddhist activity (ranging from the third century BCE to the twelfth century CE). As well as early statues of the Buddha and other symbols of the dharma (lotuses, a stupa, the bodhi tree), they include statues of Tara and the bodhisattva Padmapani from the settlement's later history as a center of Mahayana teachings.

Amravati is now a small, peaceful village, to which come a stream of pilgrims and other visitors. It stands on the banks of the Krishna River in Andra Pradesh. To get there, pilgrims can travel by train to the nearby city of Vijaywada, though this is a fairly grueling journey from Delhi (two days). From Vijaywada, the most reliable route is to go by bus to the smaller city of Guntur (an hour's journey or less), and then take a second bus from there to Amravati (a further one and a half hours); the site and museum are about a kilometer from the bus stand. During the monsoon, when the river is high, boat tours also run frequently to Amravati from Vijaywada.

The Ajanta and Ellora Caves

The Buddhist caves of Ajanta are 107 kilometers northeast of the city of Aurangabad. These magnificent caves, cut in the wall of a gorge, were begun in the fourth century CE, and have been designated a UNESCO World Heritage Site. The twenty-nine caves comprise both shrines and monasteries, and are decorated with elaborate sculptures and paintings.

The Ellora caves, just outside Aurangabad, comprise Hindu and Jain caves as well as Buddhist caves, and thus reflect the religious tolerance of India in the period from the fifth to tenth century CE, when the caves were carved. The Buddhist caves were the earliest made.

DHAULI HILL

Dhauli Hill, some eight kilometers from the city of Bhubaneshwar in Orissa, is reputedly the place where the emperor Ashoka turned away from war to embrace Buddhism. Edicts of the emperor are inscribed on a rock on the hill; a Shanti Stupa (peace pagoda) was built on the opposite hill by Fuji Guruji, a Zen Buddhist priest.

Nagarjuna Konda

The settlement of Nagarjuna Konda, in the Nalgonda district of Andhra Pradesh, is believed to have been the largest Buddhist center in South India in the early centuries of the Christian era. The site is believed to take its name from its association with Nagarjuna, who lived in the second century CE, and who developed the concept of emptiness (shunyata). Nagarjuna Konda was the capital of the Ishvaku dynasty (225-325 CE), who were Buddhists and sponsored the building of monasteries and temples.

The importance of Nagarjuna Konda as an early center of Buddhism was established by English archaeologists who excavated the site in the years 1927-1931, discovering the remains of more than thirty monasteries. The archaeological evidence suggests that the settlement had links with Buddhist centers in Bengal, Ceylon and China. The original site was flooded by damming of the Krishna river to create a reservoir for irrigation in 1960, but archaeologists moved the remains of Nagarjuna Konda to the top of a hill in the lake, where a museum now stands.

The body of Nagarjuna is believed to still be there, protected by eight female spirits.

Once, a young prince who coveted his father's kingdom, was told by his mother that he could never become king until Nagarjuna died, since Nagarjuna and the king have the same lifespan. His mother said to ask Nagarjuna for his head and since Nagarjuna was so compassionate, he would undoubtedly agree to give it to him. Nagarjuna did in fact agree, but the prince could not cut his head off with a sword. Nagarjuna said in a previous life he had killed an ant while cutting grass. As a karmic result, his head could only be cut off with a blade of kusha grass. The prince tried and at the first stroke the masters' head fell on the ground. Milk not blood poured out and the severed head spoke: "I shall now go to Tushita heaven, but later I shall return in this very same body." Afraid, the prince, threw the head far away. However, both the head and body of Nagarjuna turned into stone and it is said that the head, slowly but surely, moves closer to its trunk and that eventually, when the two reunite, Nagarjuna will revive and perform vast deeds for the benefit of the doctrine and beings.

Tso Pema

Tso Pema or Rewalsar, near the town of Mandi in Himachal Pradesh, is one of the holiest sites for Varjayana Buddhists in India. The beautiful lake, high in the Himalayan foothills is sacred to Padmasambhava or Guru Rinpoche, the great master who brought Vajrayana Buddhism to Tibet.

The lake was created by Padmasambhava in the eight century during the reign of King Shastradhara of Zahor. Princess Mandarava the daughter of Shastradhara was born possessing the marks of a dakini, innerly she had excellent qualities of virtue, compassion and worldly renunciation, outerly she was extremely beautiful, confident and charismatic. Due to her noble qualities and beauty many kings and princes sought her hand in marriage and offered huge dowries. Princess Mandarava had no desire to follow a worldly path and wished to dedicate her life to contemplation and solitude. She persistently requested her parent's permission to retire from the royal palace, after many requests the king and queen of Zahor unhappily granted Princess Mandarava's wish to leave the royal palace and enter into solitude.

Padmasambhava through his divine vision discerned that it was the appropriate time for the dissemination and teaching of the holy dharma in the kingdom of Zahor.

During Princess Mandarava's time of retreat, Padmasambhava manifested in the space above her. The princess recognizing Padmasambhava as a divine manifestation offered many prostrations and mandalas to the master and prayed for teachings and instructions. Padmasambhava accepted her request and began to instruct her in the profound inner practices of the Vajrayana.

During this time a Buffalo herder searching for a lost animal accidentally stumbled upon the site of Mandarava's retreat, hearing a man's voice the buffalo herder crept closer and saw a man's figure in the Princess's retreat.

Later the Buffalo herder remarked that he had seen a man within Princess Mandarava's retreat. Slowly a rumour spread that Princess Mandarava had foregone her celibacy and solitude. Eventually the rumour reached the king and the royal court. In a fit of extreme anger at his daughter's apparent infidelity, the king of Zahor ordered his ministers and soldiers to capture Padmasambhava and Princess Mandarava and to punish them as cruelly as possible.

Padmasambhava and Mandarava were bound by sharp, painful thorny rope and were dragged down the mountain to face the king. Shastradhara ordered that Mandarava be thrown into a prison made of the sharpest thorns and that Padmasambhava be burnt alive. The King ordered all his subjects to gather wood and oil, and then Padmasambhava, still tied up, was placed on the funeral pyre and set alight.

The massive Padmasambhava statue under construction in the hills overlooking Tso Pema, begun by Lama Wangdor Rinpoche.

The smoke from Padmasambhava's cremation pyre covered the whole valley for weeks. As the master's cremation smoke had not dissipated the King sent a minister to investigate. Upon arriving the minister found that the cremation smoke had changed into a vast clear lake and that the cremation flames had transformed into a beautiful lotus. When he heard, the king did not believe it and came with the royal court to witness the miraculous transformation. Shastradhara saw Padmasambhava sitting on a beautiful lotus in the middle of a pure clear lake. The master, serene and untouched by the flames was surrounded by a vast entourage of dakinis, appearing in their midst was no other then the beautiful Princess Mandarava.

King Shastradhara realising his mistake, cried out in regret so intense he fainted. Upon awaking the king prostrated many times and confessed to the Omniscient One. Shastradhara then offered his entire kingdom and all his subjects including Princess Mandarava as a mandala to Padmasambhava. In this way the

Princess became the great master's inseparable consort and all the people of the kingdom of Zahor became disciples. After this Padmasambhava became known as Guru Chime Pemajugne, the Immortal Lotus Born Guru. Through Padmasambhava's teachings and vast compassion, all the people of the kingdom of Zahor gained liberation.

Rewalsar is reached by local buses that frequently leave the bus station in Mandi. There are excellent guest-houses near the lake; several, run by monasteries, are almost on the water. The calm, sheltered lake is conducive to contemplation; it is said that if you stand on the shore and one of the floating islands of reeds drifts towards you, you are being visited by Padmasambhava's spirit.

A small community of monks and nuns live and meditate in caves and huts, festooned with prayer flags, on the ridge high above the lake. A local bus leaves for the caves each morning from the main street of Rewalsar. Prayer flags mark the main cave, where Padmasambhava and Mandarava are said to have meditated, and which is now a public shrine. The cave is divided into three sections. The first contains many Buddha images in a glass-enclosed altar. The second holds an enormous golden statute of Padmasambhava himself. The third section holds more small Buddha images and tsatsas (small devotional stupas molded from clay).

Visitors to the caves can make a donation to the Padmasambhava project, which aims to construct a huge seated image of Guru Rinpoche in a temple sited above the lake. If you miss the return bus, which leaves early in the afternoon, it is more pleasant anyway to walk down the paths and flights of steps that lead back to the lake, through farmyards and gardens.

Dharamsala

When Buddhists refer to Dharamsala they are generally thinking of McLeod Ganj or Upper Dharamsala, the suburb of Dharamsala perched on the crest of a ridge high above the rest of the town, where a substantial Tibetan community has sprung up around the residence of His Holiness the Dalai Lama. His Holiness the Seventeenth Karmapa also resides only ten kilometers along the Kangra Valley from Lower Dharamsala, at Gyuto Tantric University. Numerous other Tibetan Buddhist monasteries are situated in the Kangra Valley within a few hours' drive of Dharamsala, so McLeod Ganj is an excellent base for a student of Buddhism wishing to attend teachings and learn Tibetan. McLeod Ganj has many excellent guest-houses, several of them run by monasteries, while for a long-term stay a student can rent rooms in a Tibetan household at a modest rate.

The Kangra District was annexed by the British in 1848, and Dharamsala was founded as the base of a native regiment in 1849, and became the administrative center of the district in 1852. Because of its altitude (lower Dharamsala is at about 1200 meters, and McLeod Ganj at 1700 meters), the town became popular as a hill station, to which British households would retire from the plains during the hot summer months. A huge earthquake in 1905 largely destroyed the town and nearby Kangra, killing approximately 20,000 people. After this the summer capital of the British Raj was moved to Shimla.

When Tenzin Gyatso, the fourteenth Dalai Lama, fled Tibet at the time of the Tibetan uprising in 1959, Prime Minister Nehru allowed His Holiness to settle in Dharamsala in 1960 and set up the Tibetan Government in Exile. Over the years thousands of Tibetans have settled in the town, which contains numerous important Tibetan political and cultural institutions, including the Tibetan Institute of Performing Arts, the Central Institute of Higher Tibetan Studies, Tibetan Children's Villages, and the residence of the Tibetan State Oracle.

His Holiness's residence stands on a point of land jutting out from the ridge of McLeod Ganj, beside the main gompa of the community, and many residents circumambulate the residence each day. The Lingkor circuit is a paved track with lines of prayer wheels and large individual prayer wheels in several places, and is set with stones carved with Om Mani Peme Hung and other mantras.

His Holiness's busy schedule of visits and teachings in other countries and elsewhere in India means that he is away for much of the year, but each year he also gives teachings in Dharamsala, and it is still possible to meet him briefly in person: pilgrims must first go through a security clearance process. It is not certain how much longer this will be possible, however, as spokespeople for the Dalai Lama have indicated that he is considering retirement, which may involve moving to a remote monastery in the Himalayas.

A visit to Dharamsala also offers the opportunity to attend teachings by His Holiness Orgyen Trinley Dorje, the Seventeenth Karmapa. His Holiness resides at Gyuto Tantric University in Sidbhari, about ten kilometers from Lower Dharamsala, and gives daily public audiences including teachings on Wednesday and Saturday when he is in residence. These audiences are generally held at 2.30 pm, though it is advisable to arrive early, allowing time for the security checks. Buses to Gyuto Tantric University leave frequently from the bus station at the bottom of the main street of Lower Dharamsala.

As well as the chance to see and hear these great teachers, Dharamsala offers students the opportunity to deepen and enrich their knowledge of Buddhism by attending courses, learning Tibetan and associating with the Tibetan community. Beginners' and advanced courses in Buddhism are offered at the Institute of Higher Tibetan Studies and at some monasteries in McLeod Ganj. Visitors can enroll in formal courses in Tibetan language, or receive private tuition at modest rates. Gu-Chu-Sum, the center for Tibetan refugees who have been political prisoners, welcomes the assistance of westerners who are willing to provide one on one tuition in English to the center's residents.

Although McLeod Ganj offers every amenity, pilgrims should take care for their safety, particularly when walking outside the town or at night.

Gyuto University— Temporary Residence of His Holiness Karmapa

Gyuto Ramoche Tantric University, outside Dharamsala, India, nestled in the foothills leading to the Himalayan mountain range has been the temporary residence of His Holiness the seventeenth Gyalwa Karmapa, Ogyen Trinley Dorje since escaping from Tibet in 2000.

When in residence at his temporary camp at the Gyuto Tantric University in the Dharamsala area, His Holiness's schedule is typically very tight since he is devoting almost all of his time to studies, which include the process of transmission and empowerment from his teachers, as well as Buddhist philosophy and meditation practice.

However, His Holiness has earmarked a portion of his time for public audiences and has a limited amount of time for private audiences. When his travel and study schedule permits, His Holiness holds public audiences in Sidbhari at Gyuto Tantric College, for which prior appointments are not necessary. The public audiences usually include a brief teaching granted during the audience time.

For further information visit www.kagyuoffice.org

Palpung Sherabling—
Seat of Kenting Tai Situpa

Palpung Sherabling Monastic Seat is situated in the northern Indian Province of Himachal Pradesh, about 530 km away from Delhi and about 2 1/2 hours drive west from Dharamsala.

In 1975, the present twelfth Kenting Tai Situpa's disciples from Derge and Nangchen region who settled in Bir, Himachal Pardesh Northern India, donated a protected pine forested land located in the foothills of the Himalayas. Here Kenting Tai Situpa started to establish Palpung Sherabling, which later became his seat in India. The building was designed by Kenting Tai Situpa, and is built of modern materials and finished in traditional Tibetan architectural fashion. The concept of the design follows the ancient science of geomancy. Palpung Sherabling cultivates and preserves the artistic lineage of the Palpung tradition. The monastery, only a few miles from the nearest town, retains its calmness and isolation.

It has 250 monks' quarters, (which accommodate over 500 monks) three shrine halls, six shrine rooms, and all of the traditional and modern monastic features. Palpung Sherabling also has retreat houses for monks and nuns and individual cabins for lay practitioners.

Kenting Tai Situpa is progressively developing Palpung Sherabling according to his ideal: from an ordinary point of view, to build a seat for a great master; from a more profound level to establish a place to display and maintain the culture and lineage of Tibetan Buddhism and a place to educate the masters of the next generation; from the foremost and most profound level, to transform this pure land into the Wisdom Deities' Mandala.

A recent addition has been Palpung International Institute of Buddhist Studies, which provides accommodation facilities for students coming to Palpung Sherabling for the many dharma courses from the lineage masters. This project is managed and supervised by Venerable Thutop Rinpoche.

For further information visit www.palpung.org

BOUDHANATH STUPA

There are a variety of accounts as to who founded the great stupa at Boudhanath in the Kathmandu Valley and when, and what relics it may contain. It is one of the largest ancient stupas in the world, and the main center of Buddhist pilgrimage and Tibetan Buddhist culture in Nepal.

The stupa is said to house relics of Kashyapa, the Buddha who achieved enlightenment and taught the dharma before Buddha Shakyamuni. Others believe that the dome contains a fragment of bone from the cremation of Shakyamuni. The stupa is also said to have been constructed in the time of the Tibetan King Songsten Gampo (c. 600 CE), one of whose wives was the Nepalese princess Bhrikuti. Other accounts associate the raising of the stupa with the Tibetan King Trisong Detsän (755-797 CE). Some Nepalese sources attribute its foundation to the Licchavi King Sivadeva (c. 590-604 CE), others to King Manadeva (464-505 CE).

According to the Tibetan/Vajrayana tradition, Boudhanath Stupa was built by a poor elderly lady named Jhazima Demchok and her four sons who were amongst the poorest people in the kingdom. Jhazima's sons were all born from different fathers but lived together with their elderly mother. Jhazima gave rise to the aspiration to construct a Dharmadhatu Stupa so that all beings could pay homage and accumulate merit.

When Jhazima requested the king for land to build the stupa, the king was amazed and inspired by her great aspiration and immediately granted her request. As the stupa was built and word of the poor family's great effort slowly spread, the local ministers repeatedly asked the king to stop the construction of the Dharmadhatu Stupa. The ministers were fearful of their reputations as they held positions of great power and wealth and yet a poor elderly woman and her four sons were managing to benefit all beings while they could not. The king replied to his ministers that once his permission was given it could not be taken back. From this statement, the Tibetan name for the Boudhanath Stupa is derived. The Tibetan name, Ja-Rung Ka-Shor can be translated as; permission once given can't be given back.

The family and five helpers worked tirelessly for four years in the construction of the main body of the stupa. When Jhazima realised that she would not see the stupa fully completed in her lifetime, she gave instructions that upon finishing the stupa a relic of the Tathagatas must be placed inside and that extensive offerings and consecration ceremonies be completed. She stated that if they did so then they would have fulfilled all her wishes and aspirations and those of the Tathagata's of the three times.

Seven more years passed and finally the Dharmadhatu Stupa was completed. During the extensive consecration ceremonies large amounts of Kashyapa Buddha's relics were placed inside the stupa. During the ceremonies when showers of flower petals were offered to the stupa's consecration, Kashyapa Buddha and the Buddhas of the ten directions all manifested and simultaneously emitted great streams of blessings which were absorbed into the stupa and completed the consecration ceremony.

Through the immense blessing of all the Tathagatas the Boudhanath stupa became a glorious seeing liberation stupa, which grants all wishes and aspirations made before it by all beings.

The fours sons then stood before the wish fulfilling stupa and all gave rise to the noble aspiration to benefit the flourishing of dharma in the Land of Snow (Tibet).

Before the wish fulfilling stupa, the eldest son whose father was a horse herder, gave rise to the aspiration to assist the flourishing of the dharma by being born as a dharma king. He was later born as Trisong Detsun the great dharma king who introduced the teachings of Lord Buddha to the Land of Snow.

Before the wish fulfilling stupa, the second son whose father was a pig farmer, gave rise to the aspiration to assist the flourishing of dharma by being born as a great scholar. He was later born in India as Khenpo Bodhisattva, the Great Abbott of Nalanda, who crossed the Himalayas and established the monastic tradition in the Land of Snow.

Before the wish fulfilling stupa, the third son whose father was a dog keeper, gave rise to the aspiration to assist the future of dharma by being born from a lotus as a great mantra holder, he was later born at Lake Danakosha as Padmasambhava, the Vajrayana Buddha. Padmasambhava pacified all obstacles to the dissemination of dharma in The Land of Snow.

Before the wish fulfilling stupa, the fourth son whose father was a bird keeper, rejoiced at his brother's noble wishes and gave rise to the aspiration to assist the flourishing of dharma by bringing all the brothers together again in their next life. He was later born as Yalung Wami Trizhe, a minister of King Trisong Detsun. He was the king's messenger and helped to reunite all the brothers and caused the flourishing of the glorious teachings of the Vajrayana throughout The Land of Snow.

After witnessing the noble brother's pure aspirations, all the Buddhas and bodhisattvas simultaneously granted their blessing so that the son's aspirations would be fulfilled.

As with other ancient stupas, the very large mound we see today probably covers smaller, older stupas on the same site: the current stupa was built after the invasions of the Mongols in the fourteenth century CE.

As with the stupa at Swayambunath, the base of the Boudhanath stupa is a massive whitewashed hemispherical mound topped by a square stone harnika painted on all four sides with the awareness eyes of the Buddha. Above the harnika are thirteen levels symbolizing the stages of the path to enlightenment, with above that the gilded metal spire; the total height of the structure is thirty-six meters. The structure and surrounding buildings are strung with hundreds of prayer flags fluttering in the Himalayan winds. The base of the stupa mound contains 108 niches in each of which stands an image of Buddha Amitabha, and at most times of day there are people circumambulating the mound and turning the prayer wheels at its base.

The stupa stands on an ancient trade route between Nepal and Tibet, and is traditionally a place where those traveling over the Himalayas make offerings either at the start of the journey, or at the end of it to give thanks for their safe passage. The original trade route passes the Boudhanath stupa and continues to the smaller and almost certainly older stupa of Chabahil, also referred to as 'Little Boudhanath', some three kilometers to the west. The Chabahil stupa is said to have been raised by Charumati, the daughter of the Buddhist emperor Ashoka. It dates from the Licchavi period—the fifth to eighth centuries CE.

With the crushing of the Tibetan uprising against the Chinese invaders in 1959, many Tibetan refugees settled at Boudhanath, eleven kilometers northeast of central Kathmandu. The place became a center for the renaissance of Tibetan Buddhism outside Tibet and the study of Vajrayana Buddhism by western students. Boudhanath today has some fifty gompas and study centers, many of which offer teachings and meditation courses, and large numbers of guest houses to accommodate the transient population of tourists and serious students of Buddhism.

SWAYAMBUNATH STUPA

Along with the great stupa at Boudhanath, the Swayambunath stupa is the other main site of Buddhist pilgrimage in Kathmandu. It is splendidly situated on a hill two kilometers to the west of the Thamel district of Kathmandu, beyond the Vishnumati River, with views out over the city and, on clear days, the mountains. Most visitors choose to approach the stupa by climbing the great stairway from the base of the hill, which was built by King Pratap Malla in the seventeenth century CE. The King also made the giant stone dorje (vajra) at the top of the staircase and the two shikaras (towers) that flank the approach to the stupa. Pilgrims who cannot manage this climb can be driven to the stupa precinct. The ascent of the stairway may involve interactions with the monkeys who inhabit the hill (tourists often refer Swayambunath as the 'the monkey temple'): it is best not to carry food, as the monkeys will try to snatch it.

There are different accounts of the origin of the stupa. The Kathmandu valley was once a lake, upon it a radiant lotus flower manifested. (Geology confirms that the valley was a lake and that the Swayambunath hill may have been an island standing in it.) The lotus stamen was blessed by all the Tathagatas and through this was spontaneously transformed into a stupa of the dharmadhatu which radiated light in the ten directions. The bodhisattva Manjushri perceived the miraculous stupa in a vision while engaged in samadhi. Manjushri manifested at the lake and to enable other beings to reach the seeing liberation stupa, cut a passage through the mountains around the valley, the water draining away left the present day Kathmandu valley. The lotus petals then transformed into the hill upon which the dharmadhatu stupa stands. The present day stupa is built over the original self arising stupa and it contains the relics of Kashyapa, the third Buddha. The Swayambunath stupa is called Rung-Jung chorten in Tibetan, which means the self arising stupa.

Another account has it that the stupa was built over an eternal, self-created (*svyambu*) flame—hence its name. The Buddhist emperor Ashoka is said to have visited Swayambunath. Moslem invaders broke open the stupa mound in the hope of finding gold in 1346.

A partially obliterated stone inscription found at the site indicates that the stupa was founded by King Vrsadeva at the beginning of the fifth century CE, and that work was carried out on the site by his great grandson King Manadeva (464-505 CE). Hindus as well as Buddhists revere Swayambunath—it has been maintained by a long series of Hindu kings of Nepal including King Pratap Malla in the seventeenth century—and the stupa precinct includes several Hindu shrines, most notably a small pagoda style temple to Hariti, the goddess of fertility and smallpox.

As with Boudhanath, the pilgrim visiting Swayambunath has the opportunity to participate in a vibrant community of practice, either by joining the circumambulation of the stupa at dawn, or by staying for the daily puja at around 4.00 pm.

Notes

1. Actually there have been many Buddhas, but the one of our present time is the Buddha Shakyamuni, who was born in 563 B.C.E. in Lumbini (in present day Nepal) and died in 483 B.C.E. in Kushinagar (in present-day India).
2. The Foundation Vehicle interpretation is that the Buddha was an ordinary man who worked hard and achieved enlightenment. The Mahayana interpretation, which Thrangu Rinpoche uses, is that each of the thousand Buddhas of this eon will perform a set of twelve deeds as an example to ordinary beings and thus start a new cycle of teachings after Buddhism has disappeared from the world again each time.
3. Tushita is the place, more precisely in the sambhogakaya, which can be visited by highly accomplished masters such as Asanga. This particular realm, called a "pure realm" or the "god realm," is where the next Buddha, Maitreya, resides. It is the fourth of the six subdivisions of the desire realm of gods.
4. The Buddha was born on the border of present-day India and Nepal in Lumbini, which is actually in Nepal near Rummindei. The ruins of the palace that Buddha lived in can be visited. We know this is the correct location because the Buddhist King Ashoka, who lived in the second century B.C.E. put a pillar in Lumbini to mark the spot where the Buddha was born and grew up. This pillar says "Here was born the sage of the Shakya," which is the clan the Buddha came from.
5. According to the Mahayana he was a bodhisattva who attained Buddhahood in this lifetime, but according to the Vajrayana he had already attained Buddhahood and only showed the appearance of a bodhisattva attaining Buddhahood for the sake of beings.

6. Buddha's mother Mayadevi died just seven days after giving birth to the Buddha. Because a Brahmin named Kaundinya made a prophecy at the Buddha's birth that he would renounce the world, Buddha's father raised him in luxury and banned all things that might remind him of samsara. At sixteen the Buddha married his cousin Yashodhara. At the age of 29, just after the birth of his son, Rahula, he left the palace. One can see the ruins of this palace excavated originally by Makherji in 1899, and a modern temple was erected near this spot.

7. The Buddha left in royal garb with his charioteer Chandraka and his favorite horse Kanthaka and then stopped at a river, cut his hair which is a sign of renunciation, and took on the robe of a Shramana which is the name of the wandering religious adepts seeking enlightenment outside the formal Brahmin religious orders. He is reported to have gone to teachers Kalama of Vaishali and Rudraka Ramaputra of Rajagriha but, not satisfied by these, went to the Nairanjana River (its modern name is the Lilajan river near modern Urel) where, with five other Brahmins, he engaged in ascetic practices which led to starvation.

8. At the age of thirty-five he took the milk offered by the girl Sajata and sat under the pipal tree, which is also known as the bodhi tree, for seven weeks seeking enlightenment. This bodhi tree can be visited in the modern city of Bodhgaya in northern India, which is one of the holiest places in Buddhism, particularly the Mahabodhi stupa erected after the time of the Buddha. The original bodhi tree has died but an offspring of this tree is still there and is the object of a great deal of worship. This area was excavated by Cunningham in the 1890s and there are still railings and other stonework from the first century B.C.E.

9. The deer park in which the Buddha gave his first sermon, explaining the Four Noble Truths, is in modern-day Sarnath, which is located four miles north of the city of Varanasi in India. The deer park actually comes from a story of the Buddha, who was a Banyan deer in a previous life. In Sarnath the emperor Ashoka erected a pillar which can be seen but has been broken off. Thrangu Rinpoche's main monastery and monastic college (shedra) overlooks this deer park.

10. This may seem to be a contradiction with the statement that Buddhists don't believe in supplicating a god. Buddhists believe there are gods in that there are deities which were created by mind. But unlike theistic religions Buddhist do not believe these deities created the universe or that they can affect your individual karma by rewarding and punishing you.
11. These five were Kaundinya, Ashvajit, Baspa, Mahanaman and Bhadrika.
12. Rajgir is located about sixty-two miles south east of the modern city of Patna and still is called Rajagriha and is a holy Buddhist site. Vulture Peak at Rajgir where the Buddha first taught the teachings on emptiness was the heart of the Magadha empire of the Buddha's time. Vulture's Peak (Gridhrakuta) was a place that the Buddha often visited and which can be visited even today. The monastery of Jivakamravana that the Buddha visited has been recently excavated. At Rajgir there are two natural caves where the Buddha lived.
13. Buddhists believe that the world as we see it is not the true nature of phenomena, but rather like an illusion. A Western example would be that we could go up to a red brick wall and hit it. The wall would appear to be solid and made of a single material of hardened clay. This would be its conventional appearance. However, a physicist would tell us that actually the wall is made of billions of atoms that are moving at incredible speeds and the spaces between these atoms is so great that the "wall" is actually 99.99% space. It only appears red because human eyes see the radiation coming from these moving atoms as being "red." So we can say the apparent nature of the wall is that it is solid and red while its true nature is more like billions of silicon and oxygen atoms flying around. Buddhists about 1500 years ago examining phenomena explained this in terms of saying that all outside matter and internal thoughts were "empty" (Skt. *shunyata*) in that they did not appear as they really are. Thrangu Rinpoche often gives the example of the great meditator Milarepa, who completely realized this emptiness and was then able to do such things as put his hand right through solid rock. This feat, incidentally, has been replicated in the past ten years by the Seventeenth Karmapa, who heads the Kagyu lineage.

14. For a detail explanation of these three levels of Buddhist practice see Thrangu Rinpoche's *The Three Vehicles of Buddhist Practice* published by Namo Buddha Publications.
15. When the Buddha was 79 years old he was accompanied by Ananda and visited several places, including Nalanda, and stopped at a mango grove in Vaishali. He was taken ill and decided to die in exactly three months. He gradually went to Kushinagar and there he laid down in the "lion's position" and passed away at the age of 80. He had taught for 45 years and his last words were, "Decay is inherent in all composite things. Work out your own salvation with diligence."

    Kushinagar where the Buddha died can also be visited. The ruins of Kushinagar are situated near the town of Kasia twenty-two miles north-east of Deoria in Uttar Pradesh in India. This place has two large Buddhist monasteries located where the Buddha passed away and was cremated. One stupa where the Buddha passed away has been excavated and restored several times and contained a number of relics. There are also eight excavated monasteries nearby. Where the Buddha was cremated is a stupa about fifty feet high.
16. In fact almost all Western scholarship into early Buddhism maintains this position.
17. These ten rules were the permission of: (1) exclamations of astonishment such as "acho," (2) making exclamations of rejoicing, (3) living by agriculture, (4) to mix the sacred salt that is to be kept for a lifetime with that used in general living, (5) eating at the wrong time because one is traveling, (6) eating food that has been left from a previous meal "with two fingers," (8) taking intoxicants under pretense that it was for medical use, (9) getting a new meditation carpet without fixing the old one, and (10) begging for gold and silver.
18. These seven patriarchs were Mahakashyapa, Ananda, Upagupta, Canavasika, Dhitika, Krisna and Mahasudarchana.
19. The ruins of Nalanda lie just seven miles north of Rajgir. The location is said to have been visited several times by the Buddha and is the birth place of Shariputra. When the Chinese pilgrim Fa-hien visited

this site in the (4th century?) he saw a stupa to Shariputra there. The Chinese visitor Hiuen Tasang visited Nalanda in 637 C.E. and reports a six-story temple with an 80 foot high copper statue of the Buddha. He stayed and studied there and gave us a description of Nalanda. The remains of about a three story temple remains and one can see the walls of the monastic rooms of the monastery. The monastery was destroyed by the Muslims in the twelfth century. The site was recognized by Cunningham and has been extensively excavated. Today there are eleven monasteries uncovered and one large temple. The statues and bronzes that were recovered are in nearby museums.

20. The 84 mahasiddhas were individuals living ordinary vocations who reached high realization using Vajrayana practices. Their story is told in Keith Dowman's *The Buddha's Lions*, Berkeley: Dharma Publishing.
21. This was a Brahmin called Durdhasakala, whom Taranatha identifies with Matriceta and who according to Tibetan tradition was in fact Asvaghosha before he became a Buddhist. We will call him Matriceta.
22. Part of this story of Asanga comes from the 1988 Oxford Namo Buddha Seminar.
23. When the Buddha taught, he did not give lectures, but rather would answer questions from whomever asked him a question. As a result the Buddha had to teach persons of all different abilities and levels of understanding. Also to a person without a very sophisticated view of Buddhism, the Buddha would give approximate answers to their question which they could understand and these are called the provisional teachings. When teaching students with advanced understanding and meditational experience, the Buddha would teach the complete or final answer, and these are called the definitive teachings.
24. Thrangu Rinpoche has written an extensive commentary on four of these works namely *The Clear Ornament of Realization*, *Differentiating Dharma and Dharmata*, *Differentiating the Middle from the Extremes*, and *The Uttara Tantra*. All are available from Namo Buddha Publications.

25. The Buddha spoke the popular dialect of the time, but the teachings were put into Sanskrit by the Sarvastivada school since that was the language of scholars.
26. In India the actual form of the Buddha was represented by a lotus flower, not by a person, until about the first century C.E.
27. This has been translated as *The Marvelous Companion: Life Stories of the Buddha* by Aryasura. Berkeley: Dharma Books, 1983.
28. This happened at Namo Buddha in Nepal where Thrangu Rinpoche has his three-year retreat center and where Namo Buddha Publications gets its name.
29. This and the following three chapters were teachings given by Thrangu Rinpoche while leading a pilgrimage to the four main Buddhist holy sites on December 15 - 30, 1991. They were translated into English by Jules Levinson.
30. Adventitious means it is not an inherent part of something, so it can be easily removed. For example, dirt and grime are not an inherent part of gold, so they can be removed from gold by washing without affecting the gold in any way. In this way dirt and grime are adventitious to gold.
31. Rinpoche is referring to yidam practice which is a practice particular to the Vajrayana. Briefly, in this practice one visualizes a deity such as Chenrezig, White Tara, or Medicine Buddha during the generation state and then does the main practice. At the end one dissolves the deity into emptiness and rests in this emptiness for a while and this is called the completion stage.
32. These two paths—*drol lam* and *thap lam*—are generally followed simultaneously or alternately by the practitioner. *Drol lam,* the path of liberation, is what sometimes we refer to as formless meditation and includes Mahamudra. In this approach to meditation one relates to the mind in terms of the awareness aspect of mind.

Thap lam, the path of means or method, includes all tantric practices employing visualization, mantras, mandalas, yogas such as *the Six Dharmas of Naropa* or the *Six Dharmas of Niguma*, etc. These practices relate to mind in terms of the energy aspect of mind. By properly integrating the distorted karmic energies of one's mind, one brings about the same enlightened awareness that is reached as the fruition of the formless meditation approach of the path of liberation. The virtue of the path of liberation is that it tends to be smoother, while the path of means is that it tends to be faster; therefore, they make a good complement to each other. Neither path can be practiced properly—and in the case of the path of means it would be dangerous to do so – without the guidance of a qualified tantric master. – *Lama Tashi Namgyal*

33. Sourced from www.buddhist-temples.com.

Glossary of Terms

Abhidharma. (Tib. *chö ngön pa*) The Buddhist teachings are often divided into the Tripitaka: the sutras (teachings of the Buddha), the Vinaya (teachings on conduct,) and the Abhidharma, which are the analyses of phenomena that exist primarily as a tradition of commentary on the Buddhist teachings.

Alaya vijnana. (Tib. *kün shi nam she*) According to the Chittamatra school this is the eighth consciousness and is often called the ground consciousness or storehouse consciousness.

Anuttarayoga tantra. (Tib. *nal jor la na me pay ju*) There are four levels of the Vajrayana and anuttarayoga tantra is the highest of these. It contains the Guhyasamaja, the Chakrasamvara, the Hevajra and the Kalachakra tantras.

Arhat. "Free from four maras." The mara of conflicting emotions, the mara of the deva, the mara of death and the mara of the skandhas. The highest level of the Foundation Vehicle path. Arhat is male and arhati is female.

Bodhichitta. (Tib. *chang chup chi sem*) Literally, the mind of enlightenment. There are two kinds of bodhichitta: absolute bodhichitta, which is completely awakened mind that sees the emptiness of all phenomena, and relative bodhichitta which is the aspiration to practice the six paramitas and free all beings from the suffering of samsara. In regard to relative bodhichitta, there are also two kinds: aspiration bodhichitta and perseverance bodhichitta.

Bodhisattva. (Tib. *chang chup sem pa*) "Heroic mind." *Bodhi* means blossomed or enlightened, and *sattva* means heroic mind. Literally, one who exhibits the mind of enlightenment. Also an individual who has committed him or herself to the Mahayana path of compassion and the practice of the six paramitas to achieve Buddhahood to free all beings from samsara. These are the heart or mind disciples of the Buddha.

Bodhisattva levels. (Skt. *bhumi,* Tib. *sa*) The levels or stages a bodhisattva goes through to reach enlightenment. These consist of ten levels in the sutra tradition and thirteen in the tantra tradition. The ten are: 1. Overwhelming Joy, 2. Stainless, 3. Radiant, 4. Luminous, 5. Difficult to Practice, 6. Obviously Transcendent , 7. Far Gone, 8. Unshakeable, 9. Excellent Discriminating Wisdom, 10. Cloud of Dharma.

Bodhisattva vow. The vow to attain Buddhahood for the sake of all beings.

Buddha nature. (Tib. *de shegs nying po*) The essential nature of all sentient beings; the potential for enlightenment.

Charya tantra, is a combination of the meditative practices of the Yoga tantra with the ritual ablution of Kriya tantra.

Chittamatra school. (Tib. *sem tsampa*) A school founded by Asanga in the fourth century, usually translated as the Mind-only school. It is one of the four major schools in the Mahayana tradition (the others being the two Rangtong—Svatantrika and Prasangika—and Shentong) and its main tenet (to greatly simplify) is that all phenomena are mental events.

Completion stage. (Tib. *dzo rim*) In the Vajrayana there are two stages of meditation: the generation/development stage and the completion stage. Completion stage with marks is the six doctrines. Completion stage without marks is the practice of essence Mahamudra, resting in the unfabricated nature of mind.

Daka. (Tib. *khandro*) A male counterpart to a dakini.

Dakini. (Tib. *khandroma*) A yogini who has attained high realizations of the fully enlightened mind. She may be a human being who has achieved such attainments or a non-human manifestation of the enlightened mind of a meditational deity. A female aspect of the protectors. It is feminine energy which has inner, outer and secret meanings.

Definitive meaning. The Buddha's teachings that state the direct meaning of dharma. They are not changed or simplified for the capacity of the listener, in contrast to the provisional meaning.

Dharmadhatu. (Tib. *chö ying*) Dharma is "the truth" and dhatu means, "space free from a centre." The all-encompassing space, unoriginated and without beginning, out of which all phenomena arises. The Sanskrit means "the essence of phenomena" and the Tibetan means "the expanse of phenomena," but it usually refers to the emptiness that is the essence of phenomena. Dharmadhatu and dharmakaya are essentially the same; they are two indivisible aspects of the same thing. The dharmakaya emphasizes the wisdom aspect while dharmadhatu emphasizes the emptiness aspect.

Disturbing emotions. (Skt. *klesha*, Tib. *nyön mong*) Also called the "afflictive emotions," these are the emotional afflictions or obscurations (in contrast to intellectual obscurations) that disturb the clarity of perception. These are also translated as "poisons." They include any emotion that disturbs or distorts consciousness. The main kleshas are desire, anger and ignorance.

Dzogchen. (Skt. *mahasandhi*) Literally "the great perfection." The teachings beyond the vehicles of causation, first taught in the human world by the great vidyadhara Garab Dorje.

Emptiness. (Tib. *tong pa nyi* Skt. *shunyata*) A central theme in Buddhism. It should not lead one to views of nihilism or the like, but is a term indicating the lack of any truly existing independent nature of any and all phenomena. Positively stated, phenomena do exist, but as mere appearances, interdependent manifestations of mind with no limitation. It is not that it is just your mind, as mind is also free of any true existence. This frees one from a solipsist view. This is interpreted differently by the individual schools.

Father tantra. (Tib. *pha gyu*) There are three kinds of tantras. The *father tantra* is concerned with transforming aggression, the *mother tantra* with transforming passion, and the *non-dual tantra* with transforming ignorance,

Four Noble Truths. (Tib. *pak pay den pa shi*) The Buddha began teaching with a talk in India at Sarnath on the Four Noble Truths. These are the truth of suffering, the truth of the cause of suffering, the cessation of suffering and the path. These truths are the foundation of Buddhism.

Generation stage. (Skt. *utpattikrama*, Tib. *che rim*) In the Vajrayana there are two stages of meditation: the generation and the completion stage. The generation stage is a method of tantric meditation that involves the visualization and contemplation of deities for the purpose of purifying habitual tendencies and realizing the purity of all phenomena. In this stage visualization of the deity is established and maintained.

Hevajra tantra. (Tib. *kye dorje*) This is the "mother tantra" of the Anuttarayoga tantra, which is the highest of the four yogas.

Hinayana (Foundation Vehicle). (Tib. *tek pa chung wa*) Literally, the "lesser vehicle." The first of the three *yanas*, or vehicles. The term refers to the first teachings of the Buddha, which emphasized the careful examination of mind and its confusion. It is the foundation of Buddha's teachings focusing mainly on the four truths and the twelve interdependent links. The fruit is liberation for oneself.

Kalachakra. A tantra and a Vajrayana system taught by Buddha Shakyamuni.

Karma. (Tib. *lay*) Literally "action." The unerring law of cause and effect, e.g., positive actions bring happiness and negative actions bring suffering. The actions of each sentient being are the causes that create the conditions for birth and the circumstances in that lifetime.

Kriya tantra. (Tib. *ja way gyu*) One of the four tantras, this emphasizes personal purity.

Madhyamaka. (Tib. *u ma*) The most influential of the four schools of Indian Buddhism founded by Nagarjuna in the second century C.E. The name comes from the Sanskrit word meaning "the Middle-way" meaning that it is the middle way between eternalism and nihilism. The main postulate of this school is that all phenomena—both internal mental events and external physical objects—are empty of any true nature. The school uses extensive rational reasoning to establish the emptiness of phenomena. This school does, however, hold that phenomena do exist on the conventional or relative level of reality.

Mahakala. Dharmapala. A protector of the dharma and dharma practitioners.

Mahapandita. (Tib. *pan di ta chen po*) *Maha* means great and *pandita* Buddhist scholar.

Mahasiddha. (Tib. *drup thop chen po)* A practitioner who has a great deal of realization. *Maha* means great and *siddha* refers to an accomplished practitioner. These were particularly Vajrayana practitioners who lived in India between the eight and twelfth century and practiced tantra. The biography of some of the most famous is found in *The Eighty-four Mahasiddhas.*

Mahayana. (Tib. *tek pa chen po)* Literally, the "Great Vehicle." These are the teachings of the second turning of the wheel of dharma, which emphasize shunyata, compassion and universal Buddha nature. The purpose of enlightenment is to liberate all sentient beings from suffering as well as oneself. Mahayana schools of philosophy appeared several hundred years after the Buddha's death, although the tradition is traced to teachings he gave at Rajgir, or Vulture Peak Mountain.

Mandala. (Tib. *chil kor)* Literally "centre and surrounding" but has different contexts. A diagram used in various Vajrayana practices that usually has a central deity and four directions.

Mara. (Tib. *du)* Difficulties encountered by the practitioner. The Tibetan word means heavy or thick. In Buddhism mara symbolizes the passions that overwhelm human beings as well as everything that hinders the arising of wholesome roots and progress on the path to enlightenment. There are four kinds: *skandha-mara,* which is incorrect view of self; *klesha-mara,* which is being overpowered by negative emotions; *matyu-mara,* which is death and interrupts spiritual practice; and *devaputra-mara,* which is becoming stuck in the bliss that comes from meditation.

Mother tantra. (Tib. *ma gyu)* There are three kinds tantras: *the father tantra,* which is concerned with transforming aggression; the *mother tantra,* which is concerned with transforming passion and the non-dual tantra, which concerns transforming ignorance.

Nirvana. (Tib. *nyangde)* Literally, "extinguished." Individuals live in samsara and with spiritual practice can attain a state of liberation in which all false ideas and conflicting emotions have been extinguished. This is called nirvana. The nirvana of a Foundation Vehicle practitioner is freedom from cyclic existence as an arhat. The nirvana of a Mahayana practitioner is Buddhahood, free from extremes of dwelling in either samsara or the perfect peace of an arhat.

Sometimes it is categorized as three types: nirvana of naturalness, which is ground nirvana; nirvana of cessation, which is path nirvana; and non-abiding nirvana, which is the reward or fruition nirvana.

Oral Instructions. (Tib. *man ngag, dams ngag*) As opposed to the scholastic traditions, the oral instructions of the Practice lineages are concise and pithy so they can always be kept in mind; they are practical and to the point so they are effective means to deal directly with the practice.

Pandita. A great scholar.

Paramita. "Transcendental" or "Perfection." Pure actions free from dualistic concepts that liberate sentient beings from samsara. The six paramitas are: generosity, moral ethics, patience, diligence, meditative-concentration, and wisdom-awareness. The ten paramitas are the above six and, skillful means, aspiration, strength, and primordial wisdom.

Prajna. (Tib. *she rab*) In Sanskrit it means "perfect knowledge" and can mean wisdom, understanding or discrimination. Usually it means the wisdom of seeing things from a high (i.e., non-dualistic) point of view.

Prajnaparamita. (Tib. *she rab chi parol tu chinpa*) Transcendent perfect knowledge. The Tibetan literally means, "gone to the other side" or "gone beyond" as expressed in the Prajnaparamita mantra, "Om gate gate paragate parasamgate bodhi svaha." The realization of emptiness in the *Prajnaparamita Hridaya* or *Heart Sutra,* made possible by the extraordinarily profound dharma of the birth of Shakyamuni Buddha in the world and the practices that came from it, such as the Vajrayana tantras, which make use of visualization and the control of subtle physical energies.

Prajnaparamita sutras. Used to refer to a collection of about 40 Mahayana sutras that all deal with the realization of prajna.

Provisional meaning. The teachings of the Buddha which have been simplified or modified to the capabilities of the audience. This contrasts with the definitive meaning.

Rangtong school. The Madhyamaka or Middle-way is divided into two major schools; Rangtong (empty of self) and Shentong (empty of other). Rangtong is from the second turning of the wheel of dharma and teaches that reality is empty of self and beyond concepts.

Sadhana. (Tib. *drup tap*) Tantric liturgy and procedure for practice, usually emphasizing the generation stage.

Samsara. (Tib. *kor wa*) "Cyclic existence." The conditioned existence of ordinary life in which suffering occurs because one still possesses attachment, aggression and ignorance. It is contrasted to nirvana. Through the force of karma motivated by ignorance, desire and anger one is forced to take on the impure aggregates and circle the wheel of existence until liberation.

Sangha. (Tib. *gen dun*) "Virtuous One." *Sang* means intention or motivation and *gha* means virtuous. One with virtuous motivation. One of the Three Jewels. Generally refers to the followers of Buddhism, and more specifically to the community of monks and nuns. The exalted sangha are those who have attained a certain level of realization of the Buddha's teachings.

Secret mantra. (Tib. *sang ngak*) A name for the Vajrayana.

Shastra. (Tib. *tan chö*) The Buddhist teachings are divided into words of the Buddha and the commentaries of others on his works, the shastras.

Shentong school. The Madhyamaka or Middle-way is divided into two major schools, Rangtong (empty of self) and Shentong (empty of other). Shentong is from the third turning of the wheel of dharma and explains that ultimate reality is emptiness and luminosity inseparable.

Shravaka. "Hearer"; corresponds to the level of arhat, those that seek and attain liberation for themselves through listening to the Buddha's teaching and gaining insight into selflessness and the four truths. These are the Buddha's speech disciples.

Siddha. (Tib. *drup top*) An accomplished Buddhist practitioner.

Siddhi. (Tib. *ngodrup*) "Accomplishment." The spiritual accomplishments of accomplished practitioners. Usually refers to the "supreme siddhi" of complete enlightenment, but can also mean the "common siddhis," eight mundane accomplishments.

Skandha. (Tib. *pung pa*) Literally "heaps." The five aspects which comprise the physical and mental constituents of a sentient being: physical form, sensations, conceptions, formations and consciousness. These can also be seen from the perspective of the five basic transformations that perceptions undergo when an object is perceived. First is form, which includes all sounds, smells, etc., everything that is not thought. The second and third are sensations (pleasant and unpleasant, etc.) and their identification. Fourth are mental events, which actually include the second and third aggregates. The fifth is ordinary consciousness, such as the sensory and mental consciousnesses.

Skillful means or upaya. (Tib. *thabs*). Generally, upaya conveys the sense that enlightened beings teach the dharma skillfully, taking into consideration the various needs, abilities, and shortcomings of their students. Upaya is an expression of compassion. In the bodhisattva's discipline, it corresponds to the first five paramitas and to relative bodhichitta. By prajna alone, without upaya, the bodhisattva is fettered to a quietistic nirvana. By upaya without prajna, one remains bound to samsara. Therefore the practitioner must unify them.

In Vajrayana, upaya arises from shunyata. It is joined with prajna and represents the male, form aspect of the union of form and emptiness.

Spiritual song. (Skt. *doha*, Tib. *gur*) A religious song spontaneously composed by a Vajrayana practitioner. It usually has nine syllables per line.

Sutra. (Tib. *do*) Sometimes "sutra" is used to cover all of the teachings given by the Buddha himself. But correctly it means one of the three sections of the dharma called the Tripitaka or Three Baskets. In the Tripitaka there are the Sutras, the Vinaya and the Abhidharma. The sutras are mainly concerned with meditation or samadhi; the Abhidharma is mainly concerned with the development of wisdom and understanding; and the Vinaya is mainly concerned with discipline and the rules of morality and conduct.

Tantra. (Tib. *gyu.*) Literally, tantra means "continuity," and in Buddhism it refers to two specific things: the texts (resultant texts, or those that take the result as the path) that describe the practices leading from ignorance to enlightenment, including commentaries by tantric masters; and the way to enlightenment itself, encompassing the ground, path and fruition. One can divide Buddhism into the sutra tradition and the tantra tradition. The sutra tradition primarily involves the academic study of the Mahayana texts and the tantric path primarily involves practicing the Vajrayana practices. The tantras are primarily the texts of the Vajrayana practices.

Three sufferings. These are the suffering of suffering, the suffering of change, and pervasive suffering (meaning the inherent suffering in all of samsara).

Torma. (Tib.) A sculpture made out of tsampa and molded butter, used as a shrine offering, a feast offering substance, or as a representation of deities. There are traditional designs for each of the many types of torma.

Tushita paradise. (Tib. *gan dan*) This is one of the heaven fields of the Buddha. Tushita is in the sambhogakaya and therefore is not located in any place or time.

Vajrayana. (Tib. *dorje tek pa*) Literally, "diamond-like" or "indestructible capacity." *Vajra* here refers to method, so the method yana. There are three major traditions of Buddhism (Hinayana or Foundation Vehicle, Mahayana, Vajrayana). The Vajrayana is based on the tantras and emphasizes the clarity aspect of phenomena. A practitioner of the method of taking the result as the path.

Vinaya. One of the three major sections of the Buddha's teachings showing ethics, what to avoid and what to adopt. The other two sections are the Sutras and the Abhidharma.

Wheel of dharma. (Skt. *dharmachakra*) The Buddha's teachings correspond to three levels which very briefly are: the first turning was the teachings on the Four Noble Truths and the teaching of the egolessness of person; the second turning was the teachings on emptiness and the emptiness of phenomena; the third turning was the teachings on luminosity and Buddha nature.

Yidam. (Tib.) *Yi* means mind and *dam* means pure, or *yi* means your mind and *dam* means inseparable. The yidam represents the practitioner's awakened nature or pure appearance. A tantric deity that embodies qualities of Buddhahood and is practiced in the Vajrayana. Also called a tutelary deity.

Yoga tantra. (Tib. *naljor gyi gyu*) Literally, "union tantra" and refers to a tantra that places emphasis on internal meditations.

Index

A

Abhidharma 29-33, 35, 37, 58, 59, 62-64, 107, 168, 173
Ananda 29, 46, 48, 168, 177, 180, 188, 222
Anuttarayoga tantra 25, 38
Arhat 24, 29, 30, 32, 33, 36, 41, 46-48, 110, 111, 130, 162, 168
Arya 25, 38, 76, 110, 171
Aryadeva 55-57, 63, 80, 113, 175
Asanga 42, 58-63, 87, 113, 114, 166, 175, 189, 219, 223
Ashoka 153-159, 161, 163, 168, 171, 173, 174, 178, 180, 184, 186, 193, 194, 197, 214, 216, 219, 220
Atisha 49, 154, 162, 189

B

Bhumi 16, 228
Birupa 71
Bodhgaya 8, 83, 153, 156, 161, 162, 164, 166, 176, 178, 185, 189, 220
Bodhi tree 18, 19, 153, 161, 162, 164, 170, 195, 220

Bodhisattva level 16, 41, 54, 111, 131
Brahma 22
Buddha essence 22, 86, 87, 89, 108, 109
Buddha nature 22, 24, 61, 62, 109, 166, 228, 231, 235
Buddhahood 18-20, 24, 25, 61, 83, 85, 86, 89, 109, 119, 146, 149, 219
Buddhist council
 First council 28, 29, 31, 46
 Second council 31-33
 Third council 33, 35, 36

C

Chandragomin 76
Charya tantra 25, 38
Chittamatra 52, 53, 61
Clarity 25, 59, 61, 88, 89, 90
Completion stage 26, 224
Creation stage 75, 105

D

Daka 25
Dakini 25, 38, 200, 202
Definitive teaching 61, 223

Devadatta 19, 167
Dewachen 54
Dharmadhatu 61, 88, 89, 110, 121, 216
Dharmakaya 47, 91
Dharmakirti 55, 63, 64, 68, 77, 154, 175
Dharmapala 117, 119, 120, 154, 161, 164, 175, 189
Dharma protector 115
Dharmata 61, 109, 120, 129, 131, 223
Dignaga 63, 64, 77, 78, 175
Discriminating awareness 120, 123, 124, 126, 133
Disturbing emotion 18, 23, 52, 85, 103
Dombhi Heruka 71
Doorkeeper panditas 67, 68, 73
Dzogchen 45

E
Egolessness 110
Eight consciousnesses 120
Eight mahasiddhas 71, 73

F
Fa Hien 158, 161, 171, 173, 174, 187
Father tantras 38
First council 28, 29, 31, 46
First turning of the wheel 22-24, 44, 78, 163, 190
Five paths 109-112, 129
Five wisdoms 120

Foundation vehicle 22, 26, 37, 40-49, 51, 52, 68, 73, 219,
Four Dharmas of Gampopa 112
Four immeasurables 141, 143, 146, 149
Four Noble Truths 23, 95, 97, 99, 101-103, 105, 107, 109, 111, 113, 115, 117, 119, 121, 163, 220
Four truths 23, 24, 28, 97, 103, 137
Four thoughts 97, 102, 112

G
Gampopa 49, 112, 115, 118, 119, 120, 128
Ganges River 71
Generation stage 26, 117, 230
God realm 14, 25, 38, 219
Gunaprabha 63, 113, 175
Guru 105, 115, 116, 118, 125, 197, 200, 203
Guru Yoga 118

H
Higher realm 102, 162
Hinayana 22, 43, 44, 46, 51, 96, 104, 109, 110, 111, 137, 193
Huien Tsiang 92, 158, 159, 161, 173, 174, 178, 187

I
Indrabhuti 71

J
Jnanashri 67

K

Kagyu 11, 49, 61, 112, 221
Kalachakra 38, 80, 155, 162, 180, 194
Kangyur 65
Karma 14, 23, 44, 45, 84, 87, 98, 105, 106, 141, 164, 174, 221, 233
Karmapa 49, 61, 129, 155, 204, 206, 207, 221
Karnikavana Temple 34
Kashyapa 34, 35, 46, 49, 155, 210, 212, 216
  Mahakashyapa 29, 46, 48, 168, 180, 189, 222
King Shuddhodana 19, 182
Klesha 18, 23, 84, 85, 92, 103-111, 119, 137, 138, 229
Krisnamuniraja 78
Kriya tantra 25, 38
Kukkuripa 71
Kushinagar 20, 27, 123, 153, 156, 177, 178, 179, 191, 194, 219, 222

L

Lineage Guru 116, 118
Lower realm 20, 102, 139
Lower tantras 38
Luipa 71
Lumbini 15, 135, 156, 158, 159, 183, 219
Luminosity 25

M

Madhyamaka 52-55, 57, 63, 64, 107, 130
Mahakala 56
Mahakashyapa 29, 46, 48, 168, 180, 189, 222
Mahamudra 52, 119, 224
Mahapandita 49, 67
Mahaparanirvana 124, 156, 177, 178
Mahasiddha 42, 68-73, 154, 166, 189, 223
Mahayana 22, 26, 37- 43, 51-5, 57, 59, 61-3, 65, 67, 68, 73, 96, 103-05, 108-111, 137, 159, 193, 195, 219
Maitreya 37, 59-61, 114, 166, 179, 180, 189, 219
Mandala 71, 75, 80, 118, 201, 202, 209, 224
Manjushri 37, 38, 57, 59, 155, 216
Mara 18, 19, 46, 47, 147, 148, 161, 164
Marpa 45, 49, 112, 128
Matriceta 55-57, 80, 223
Mayadevi 15, 158, 159, 173, 220
Mental consciousness 120
Middle-way 52, 130, 163, 230, 232, 233
Milarepa 44, 45, 49, 112, 128, 221
Mother tantras 38

N

Nagarjuna 42, 54-56, 61-63, 68, 71, 72, 87, 113, 114, 175, 180, 198, 199, 230

Nairanjana 17, 180, 185, 220
Nalanda 42, 48, 49, 51, 54-58, 62, 63, 65, 67, 68, 76, 79, 80, 154, 156, 174-176, 212, 222, 223
Naropa 42, 49, 67, 112, 119, 128, 189, 224
Ngöndro 125
Nirmanakaya 91
Nirvana 23-25, 101, 102, 107-109, 123, 124, 135, 153, 155, 156, 167, 168, 177, 178, 189-192, 194

O
Oral instruction 114, 115, 143
Ordinary siddhi 116

P
Padmasambhava 15, 154, 155, 175, 200-202, 203, 212
Pandita 41, 49, 51, 67, 68, 73
Papiyan 18, 46, 47
Prajnakaramati 67
Prajnaparamita 22, 24, 54, 55, 61, 63, 104, 113, 114, 166
Pramana 64, 75, 77, 78
Prasannashila 58
Provisional teaching 61, 223

R
Rajgir 24, 29, 37, 153, 154, 156, 165, 166-169, 174, 176, 188, 190, 192, 221, 222
Rangjung Dorje 61

Rangtong 53, 228
Ratnavajra 67
Relative truth 87
Root guru 105, 116, 118

S
Sadhana 59, 106
Sakyaprabha 63, 64, 113, 175
Sambhogakaya 91, 219
Samsara 23-25, 44, 53, 85, 97-104, 108, 112, 135, 139, 220
Sangha 31, 48, 59, 115, 117, 167, 182, 183
Saptavarman 76
Saraha 71, 72
Sarnath 22, 95, 129, 137, 153, 156, 161, 163, 164, 166, 178, 190, 220
Sattapanni cave 29
Second council 31-33
Second turning of the wheel 22, 53, 57, 61, 62, 165
Secret mantra 25, 38, 65
Selflessness 97-99, 110, 138, 140
Seven patriarchs 42, 48, 49, 51, 68, 222
Shantideva 55, 138, 141, 150, 154, 175
Shantipa 67
Shastra 39-42, 48, 52, 55, 58, 59, 61, 62, 74, 76, 77, 81, 113, 200-202
Shentong 53
Shravaka 33-35, 41-43, 46, 47, 49, 103, 104

Shravasti 24, 156, 169-172
Shuddhodana 19, 182
Siddha 42, 68-73, 154, 166, 189, 223
Siddhi 69, 115-117, 233
   Ordinary siddhi 116
   Supreme siddhi 116, 233
Six ornaments 62, 63, 73, 113, 175
Six Yogas 119
Skillful means 25, 66
Spiritual song 40, 80
Sugatagarbha 89, 141
Sutras 22, 25, 30, 34, 39, 49, 51-55, 58, 61, 62, 64, 66, 80, 114, 192

T

Tantra 22, 25, 38, 39, 49, 61, 62, 65, 66, 79, 80, 89, 129, 155, 194
   Anuttarayoga tantra 25, 38
   Charya tantra 25, 38
   Father tantras 38
      Kriya tantra 25, 38
      Lower tantras 38
      Mother tantras 38
      Yoga tantra 25, 38
Tengyur 62, 65
Third council 33, 35, 36
Third turning of the wheel 24, 53, 58, 61-63
Three Jewels 115
Three Roots 115
Tilopa 42, 72, 112

Tirthika 55, 58, 67, 77, 78, 172
Torma 106, 107
Tushita 14, 25, 61, 62, 155, 156, 173, 199, 219
Twelve deeds 14, 21, 28, 39, 73, 219
Two great pillars 67
Two truths 28, 87, 97, 130
   Relative truth 87
   Ultimate truth 44, 87, 130

U

Ultimate truth 44, 87, 130
Upagupta 46, 47, 48, 222
Upali 29, 168

V

Vagishvarakirti 67
Vaishali 32, 180, 188, 190-193, 220, 222
Vajraghanta 69, 70, 71
Vajrapani 37, 38
Vajrasattva 117, 125
Vajrayana 25, 26, 37-43, 52, 64-71, 73, 97, 102, 103, 105, 112, 115-117, 119, 129, 132, 137, 141, 194, 200, 201, 211-214, 219, 223, 224
Varanasi 22, 24, 48, 51, 95, 163, 164, 220
Vasubhandu 58, 59, 62, 63, 110, 113, 175
Vasumitra 34
Vikramashila 42, 49, 67, 68, 154, 175, 189

Vinaya 29, 31-33, 35, 37, 63, 64, 79, 156, 168, 169
Vulture Peak 24, 29, 165, 221, 231

W
Wheel of dharma 21-28, 44, 53, 57, 58, 61-63, 65, 68, 73, 74, 79, 83, 91, 102, 135, 156, 163, 190
First turning of the wheel 22-24, 44, 78, 163, 190
Second turning of the wheel 22, 53, 57, 61, 62, 165
Third turning of the wheel 24, 53, 58, 61-63

Y
Yashah 32
Yidam 75, 115, 116, 117, 224
Yoga tantra 25, 38

Once these twenty six syllables are held in a dharma book, transgressions from their unmindful treatment will not arise. *from the root tantra of Manjushri*

Care of Dharma Books

Dharma books contain the teachings of the Buddha; they have the power to protect against lower birth and to point the way to liberation. Therefore, they should be treated with respect, kept off the floor and places where people sit or walk, and not stepped over. They should be covered or protected for transporting and kept in a high, clean place separate from more "ordinary" things. If it is necessary to dispose of dharma materials, they should be burned with care and awareness rather than thrown in the trash. When burning dharma texts, it is considered skilful to first recite a prayer or mantra, such as OM, AH, HUNG. Then you can visualize the letters of the text (to be burned) being absorbed into the AH, and the AH being absorbed into you. After that you can burn the texts.